THE VISUAL
DICTIONARY *of*
MILITARY
UNIFORMS

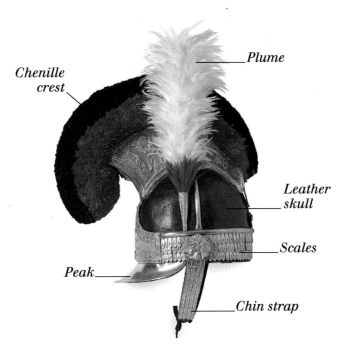

Plume

Chenille crest

Leather skull

Scales

Peak

Chin strap

BRITISH CAVALRY HELMET, c.1814

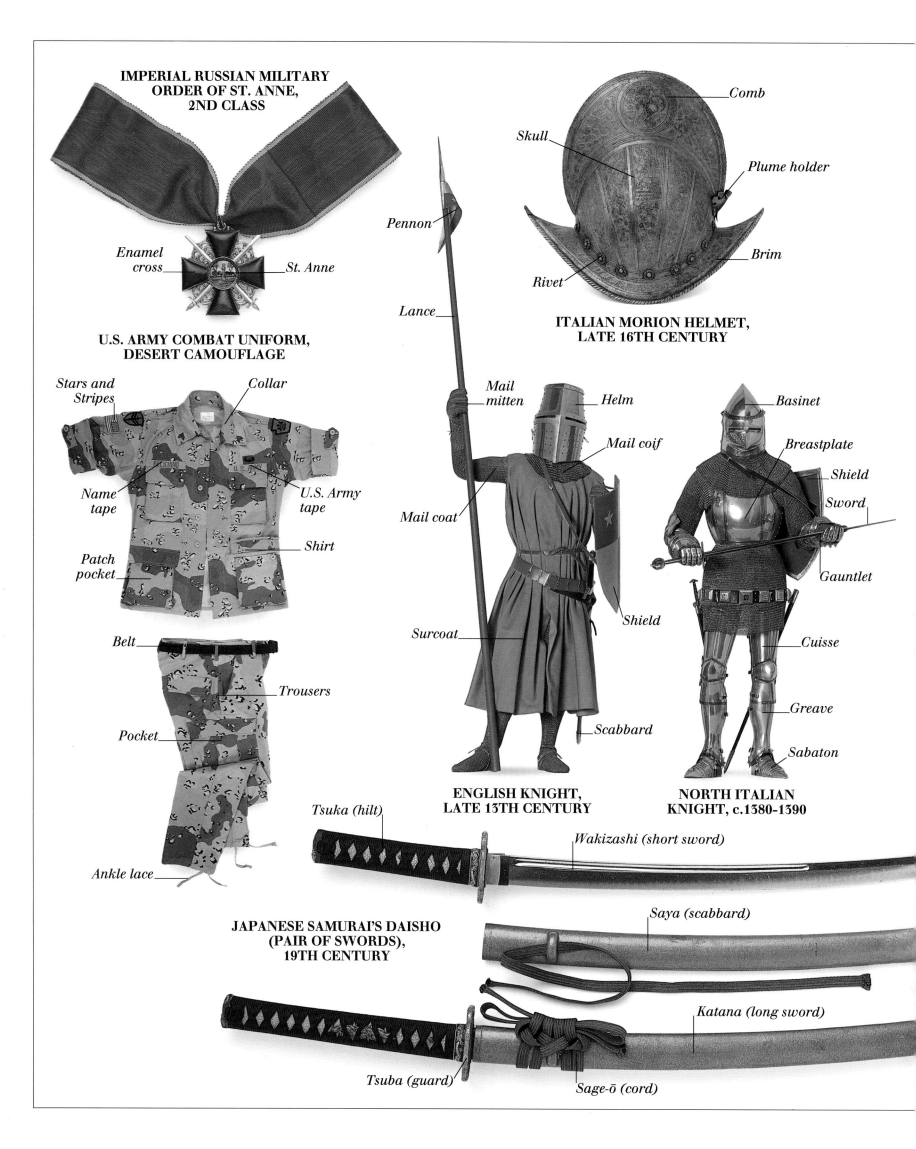

IMPERIAL RUSSIAN MILITARY ORDER OF ST. ANNE, 2ND CLASS

Enamel cross

St. Anne

U.S. ARMY COMBAT UNIFORM, DESERT CAMOUFLAGE

Stars and Stripes

Collar

Name tape

U.S. Army tape

Shirt

Patch pocket

Belt

Trousers

Pocket

Ankle lace

ITALIAN MORION HELMET, LATE 16TH CENTURY

Comb

Skull

Plume holder

Rivet

Brim

Pennon

Lance

Mail mitten

Helm

Mail coif

Mail coat

Surcoat

Shield

Scabbard

ENGLISH KNIGHT, LATE 13TH CENTURY

Basinet

Breastplate

Shield

Sword

Gauntlet

Cuisse

Greave

Sabaton

NORTH ITALIAN KNIGHT, c.1380-1390

Tsuka (hilt)

Wakizashi (short sword)

Saya (scabbard)

Katana (long sword)

JAPANESE SAMURAI'S DAISHO (PAIR OF SWORDS), 19TH CENTURY

Tsuba (guard)

Sage-ō (cord)

EYEWITNESS VISUAL DICTIONARIES

THE VISUAL DICTIONARY *of*
MILITARY UNIFORMS

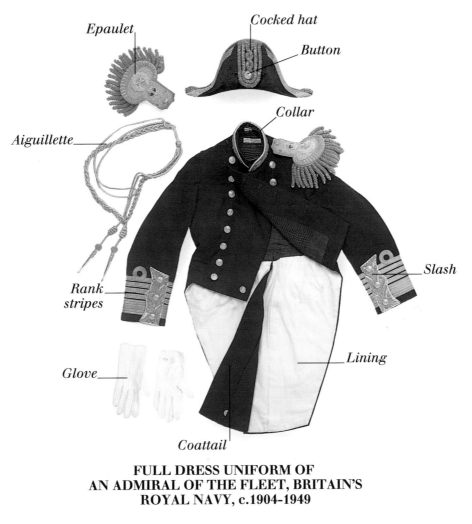

Epaulet

Cocked hat

Button

Aiguillette

Collar

Slash

Rank stripes

Glove

Lining

Coattail

**FULL DRESS UNIFORM OF
AN ADMIRAL OF THE FLEET, BRITAIN'S
ROYAL NAVY, c.1904-1949**

DORLING KINDERSLEY, INC.

NEW YORK

A DORLING KINDERSLEY BOOK

Project Art Editors Clare Shedden, Ross George
Designer Lesley Betts

Project Editor Louise Tucker
Consultant Editor Dr. Richard Holmes
U.S. Editor Charles Wills

Series Art Editors Stephen Knowlden, Paul Wilkinson
Series Editor Martyn Page
Art Director Chez Picthall
Managing Editor Ruth Midgley

Photography James Stevenson, Geoff Dann, Tim Ridley
Illustrations Ian Fleming and Associates Limited

Production Hilary Stephens

Pocket

Cocked hat

Support to hold epaulets

Epaulet

Rank insignia

Gold bullions

**ADMIRAL'S STORAGE BOX,
BRITAIN'S ROYAL NAVY, 1901-1949**

First American Edition, 1992

10 9 8 7 6 5 4 3 2 1

Dorling Kindersley Inc., 232 Madison Avenue
New York, New York 10016

Library of Congress Cataloging-in-Publication Data

Eyewitness visual dictionary of military uniforms. — 1st American ed.
p. cm. — (The Eyewitness visual dictionaries)
Includes index.
Summary: Labeled illustrations with explanatory text show the parts of various military
uniforms that have been used from ancient Roman times to the twentieth century.
ISBN 1-56458-010-5 — ISBN 1-56458-011-3
1. Military uniforms—Terminology—Juvenile literature.
2. Military uniforms—Pictorial works—Juvenile literature.
3. Picture dictionaries, English—Juvenile literature.
[1. Military uniforms.] I. Dorling Kindersley, Inc. II. Series.
UC460.E94 1992
355. 1'4'03—dc20   91–58206
                                                              CIP
                                                               AC

Reproduced by Colourscan, Singapore
Printed and bound by Arnoldo Mondadori, Verona, Italy

Contents

Cockade

Plume

Cap plate

FRENCH OFFICER'S CZAPSKA, c.1858

Otayori-no-kugi (cord stud)

Yodare-kake (throat defense)

JAPANESE SAMURAI'S MEMPO (FACE DEFENSE), 19TH CENTURY

THE ROMAN LEGIONARY 6

THE KNIGHT 8

ARMOR 10

SAMURAI WARRIOR 12

CEREMONIAL DRESS 14

HARQUEBUSIERS AND PIKEMEN 16

HEADGEAR 18

THE AMERICAN REVOLUTION 20

HUSSARS AND CARABINIERS 22

GRENADIERS AND FUSILIERS 24

EPAULETS AND INSIGNIA 26

NELSON'S NAVY 28

MEDALS AND ORDERS 30

UNION FORCES 32

CONFEDERATE FORCES 34

FOOTGEAR 36

KHAKI UNIFORMS 38

BELTS, HOLSTERS, AND SCABBARDS 40

FIRST WORLD WAR INFANTRY 42

PACKS AND GEAR 44

THE ROYAL FLYING CORPS 46

MASKS AND FACEGUARDS 48

HITLER'S ARMY 50

CAMOUFLAGE 52

WAR IN VIETNAM 54

MODERN NAVAL FORCES 56

JET AIRCREW 58

INDEX 60

ACKNOWLEDGMENTS 64

Helmet

Survival vest

Flight suit

Flight glove

Boot

U.S. HELICOPTER PILOT, c.1990

Helmet

Pauldron

Breastplate

Couter

Gauntlet

Tasset

Poleyn

GERMAN CUIRASSIER'S ARMOR, 17TH CENTURY

Loop

Lacing

Spur step

Toe cap

BRITISH OFFICER'S BOOTS, FIRST WORLD WAR (1914-1918)

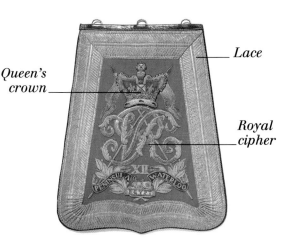

Queen's crown

Lace

Royal cipher

BRITISH CAVALRY OFFICER'S SABRETACHE, c.1840

The Roman legionary

SWORD EMBLEM

LEGIONARY INFANTRYMEN WERE the principal fighting force in the Roman army. They fought in disciplined formations and were well armed and protected. The typical legionary was armed with a javelin (pilum), a short sword (gladius), a dagger (pugio), and carried a shield (scutum). He wore a helmet (galea), a cuirass (lorica segmentata) over a woolen tunic, an apron, and sandals (caligae). The cuirass was made up of overlapping iron plates riveted to internal leather straps; at the neck and hips the edges were turned for the wearer's comfort. An embossed apron hanging from the belt protected the groin. There were many styles of helmet, including the Imperial Gallic type, which shielded the head, cheeks, and neck. Greaves (ocreae) were worn on ceremonial occasions. Auxiliary cavalrymen, widely recruited outside Italy, used long swords (spathae) and often wore mail shirts.

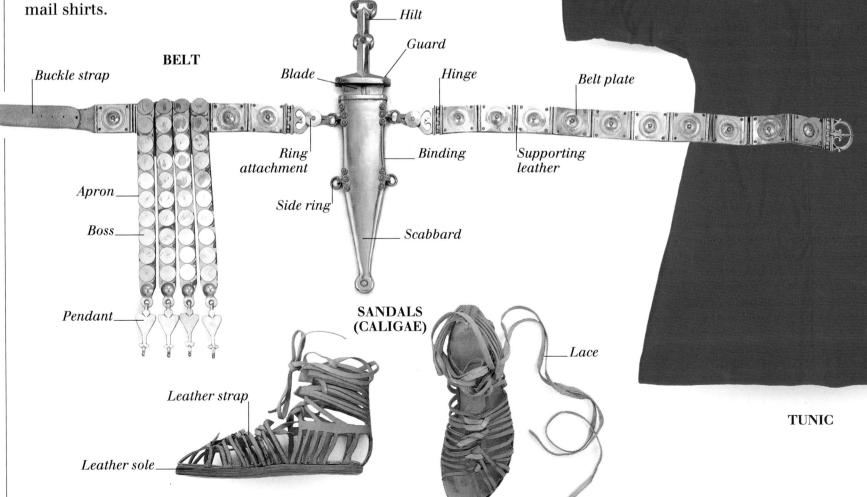

Spear (hasta)
Mail shirt
Helmet (galea)
Cheek piece
Neck flange
Pommel
Tunic
Sword (spatha)
Sandal (caliga)

AUXILIARY CAVALRYMAN, 2ND CENTURY A.D.

Neck flange
Shoulder plate
Javelin (pilum)
Sword (gladius)
Apron
Pendant
Imperial Gallic helmet
Cheek piece
Sword strap (balteus)
Cuirass (lorica segmentata)
Belt
Dagger (pugio)
Tunic
Sandal (caliga)

LEGIONARY, 1ST CENTURY A.D.

Sleeve

DAGGER (PUGIO)

Hilt
Guard
Blade
Hinge
Belt plate
Ring attachment
Binding
Supporting leather
Side ring
Scabbard

BELT

Buckle strap
Apron
Boss
Pendant

SANDALS (CALIGAE)

Leather strap
Leather sole
Lace

TUNIC

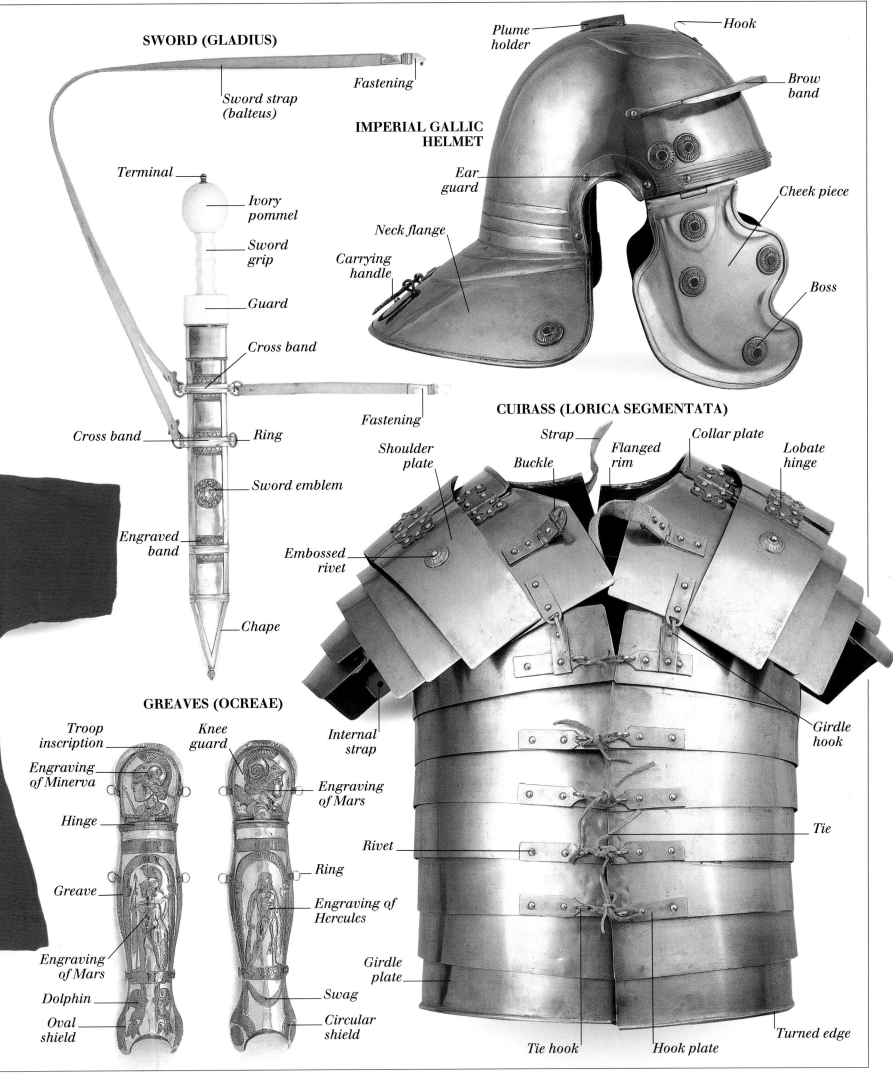

SWORD (GLADIUS)

Fastening

Sword strap
(balteus)

Terminal

Ivory
pommel

Sword
grip

Guard

Cross band

Cross band

Ring

Fastening

Sword emblem

Engraved
band

Chape

IMPERIAL GALLIC HELMET

Plume
holder

Hook

Brow
band

Ear
guard

Cheek piece

Neck flange

Carrying
handle

Boss

CUIRASS (LORICA SEGMENTATA)

Strap

Flanged
rim

Collar plate

Shoulder
plate

Buckle

Lobate
hinge

Embossed
rivet

Girdle
hook

Internal
strap

Tie

Rivet

Girdle
plate

Turned edge

Tie hook

Hook plate

GREAVES (OCREAE)

Troop
inscription

Knee
guard

Engraving
of Minerva

Engraving
of Mars

Hinge

Ring

Greave

Engraving of
Hercules

Engraving
of Mars

Dolphin

Swag

Oval
shield

Circular
shield

The knight

THE ARMORED KNIGHT ON HORSEBACK dominated the battlefields of western Europe in the Middle Ages. His supremacy was largely due to protective armor, which evolved over the centuries in response to changes in weaponry and fighting tactics. Between the 11th and 13th centuries, knights wore mail (armor made up of metal links), which was reinforced by metal plates (lames) in the 14th century. As lance charges became more common in the 15th and 16th centuries, knights needed the protection of a full suit of plate armor, such as the light field armor shown here. Made in England in about 1585, this suit of armor represents the full flowering of the armorer's craft, being beautifully decorated and also highly practical. The basic armor gave a high degree of protection, and it could be adapted for heavy fighting by fitting the falling buff in front of the faceguard and by attaching the reinforcing breastplate over the existing one.

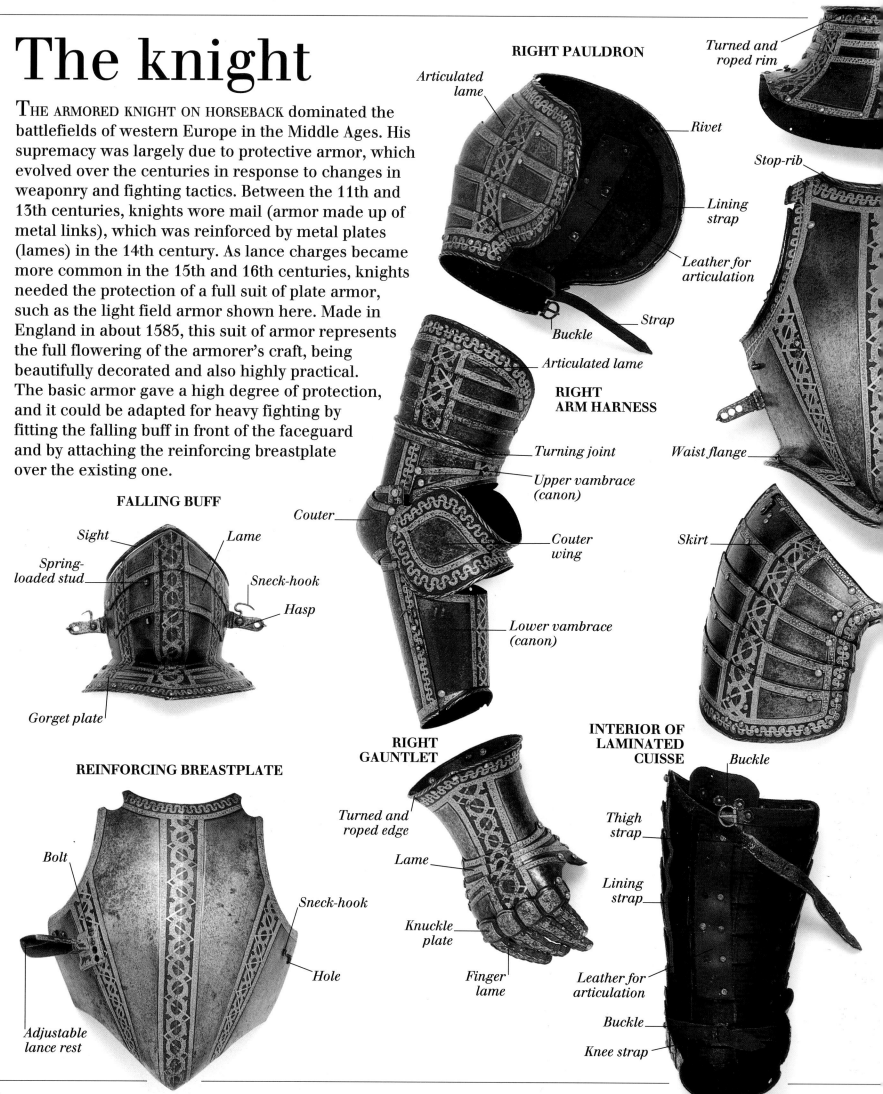

RIGHT PAULDRON

Articulated lame

Turned and roped rim

Rivet

Stop-rib

Lining strap

Leather for articulation

Strap

Buckle

Articulated lame

RIGHT ARM HARNESS

Turning joint

Upper vambrace (canon)

Counter

Couter wing

Lower vambrace (canon)

Waist flange

Skirt

FALLING BUFF

Sight

Lame

Spring-loaded stud

Sneck-hook

Hasp

Gorget plate

REINFORCING BREASTPLATE

Bolt

Sneck-hook

Hole

Adjustable lance rest

RIGHT GAUNTLET

Turned and roped edge

Lame

Knuckle plate

Finger lame

INTERIOR OF LAMINATED CUISSE

Buckle

Thigh strap

Lining strap

Leather for articulation

Buckle

Knee strap

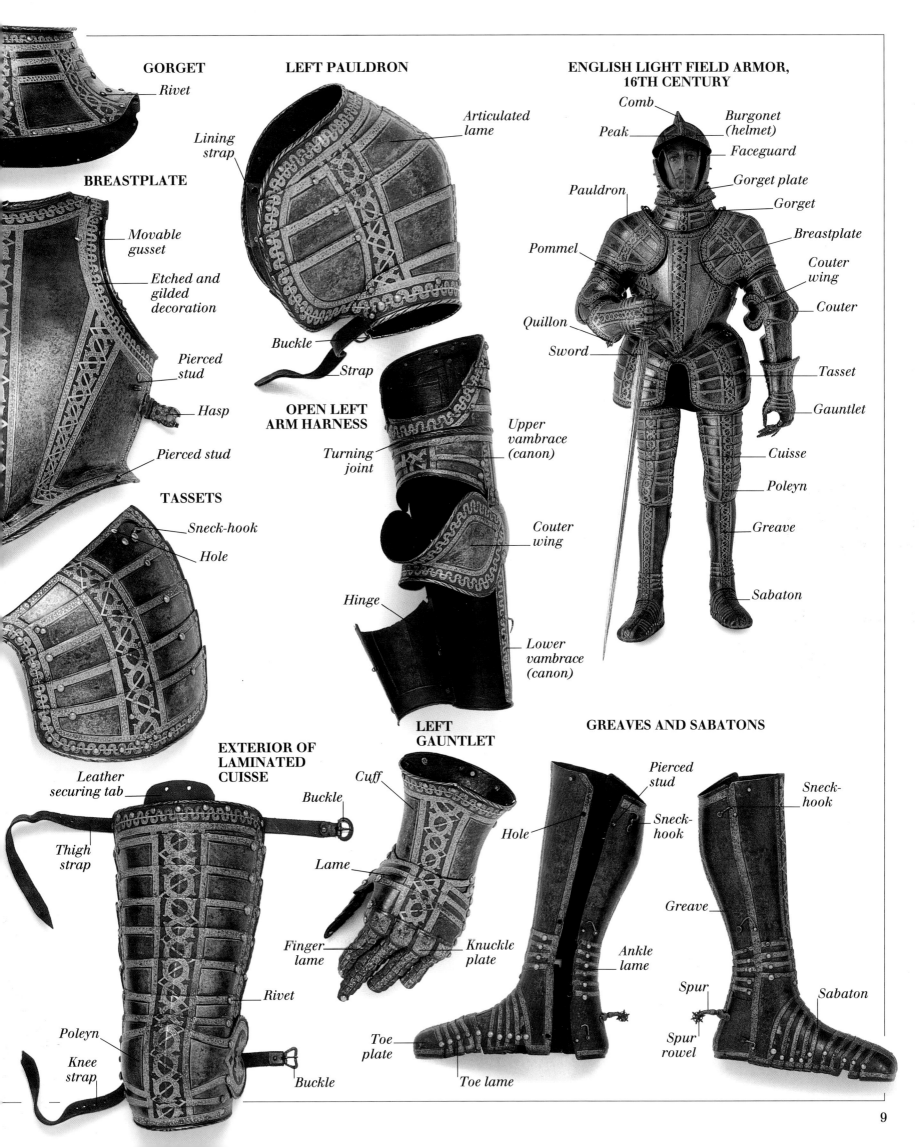

GORGET
- Rivet

BREASTPLATE
- Movable gusset
- Etched and gilded decoration
- Pierced stud
- Hasp
- Pierced stud

TASSETS
- Sneck-hook
- Hole

LEFT PAULDRON
- Lining strap
- Articulated lame
- Buckle
- Strap

OPEN LEFT ARM HARNESS
- Turning joint
- Upper vambrace (canon)
- Couter wing
- Hinge
- Lower vambrace (canon)

ENGLISH LIGHT FIELD ARMOR, 16TH CENTURY
- Comb
- Peak
- Burgonet (helmet)
- Faceguard
- Gorget plate
- Pauldron
- Gorget
- Pommel
- Breastplate
- Couter wing
- Couter
- Quillon
- Sword
- Tasset
- Gauntlet
- Cuisse
- Poleyn
- Greave
- Sabaton

EXTERIOR OF LAMINATED CUISSE
- Leather securing tab
- Buckle
- Thigh strap
- Lame
- Finger lame
- Knuckle plate
- Rivet
- Poleyn
- Knee strap
- Buckle

LEFT GAUNTLET
- Cuff
- Lame
- Finger lame
- Knuckle plate
- Toe plate
- Toe lame

GREAVES AND SABATONS
- Pierced stud
- Sneck-hook
- Hole
- Sneck-hook
- Ankle lame
- Greave
- Spur
- Spur rowel
- Sabaton

Armor

ARMOR IS ALMOST AS OLD AS WARFARE ITSELF. Garments made from leather or cloth, such as the simple Sudanese military coat (jibba) were the only protection that many soldiers had from the earliest times to the present day. However, a soldier's effectiveness in battle could be increased by providing him with armor, which was usually made partly or entirely of metal. Brigandine armor consisted of small, linked metal plates covered with cloth that might be embroidered and studded, like the Chinese coat shown here. The Indian armor is cloth reinforced with numerous studs to form a "coat of ten thousand nails." Mail armor has interwoven metal links that make it extremely flexible. It resists sword thrusts, but does little to lessen the impact of a blow. Metal plates were often worn with mail for greater protection, as in the Persian armor shown here, which combines a mail shirt with a metal breastplate. Full suits of plate armor were developed in Europe during the 15th and 16th centuries (see pp. 8-9).

INDIAN SHOULDER DEFENSE

PERSIAN ARMOR, 19TH CENTURY

- Spike
- Plume holder
- Helmet (kulah khud)
- Movable nose guard
- Mail curtain (aventail)
- Gilt metal disk
- Gilt metal studs
- Shoulder strap
- Bird's head terminal
- Mail shirt
- Breastplate (chahar ᶜaina)
- Vambrace (dastána)
- Iron mail
- Brass mail
- Mail-covered glove
- Woven gold decoration (kincob)
- Skirt
- Mail
- Cloth boot embroidered with sequins
- Sole

PERSIAN BREASTPLATE (CHAHAR ᶜAINA)

- Quilted lining
- Interior of backplate
- Shoulder strap
- Bird's head terminal
- Damascened gold decoration (koftgari)
- Edge
- Side plate
- Hinge
- Interior of side plate
- Breastplate
- Hinge pin

PERSIAN MAIL SHIRT (ZIRAH)

- Velvet-covered collar
- Sleeve
- Silk and tinsel tassel
- Edging embroidered with sequins
- Tie
- Iron mail
- Brass mail

INDIAN RAJPUT ARMOR, 18TH CENTURY

Spike

Plume holder

Helmet (tōp)

Nose guard

Mail curtain (aventail)

Matchlock musket (torador)

"Coat of ten thousand nails" (chilta hazar masha)

Sword baldric

Shoulder defense

Breastplate

Cartridge-pouch belt (kamr)

Vambrace (dastána)

Sword (khanda)

Cartridge pouch

Thigh plate

Powder flask (barutdan)

Scabbard

Armored boot (rak)

SUDANESE MILITARY COAT (JIBBA)

Sleeve

Neck opening

Pocket

Appliqué patch

Skirt

INDIAN CUIRASS OF "COAT OF TEN THOUSAND NAILS" (CHILTA HAZAR MASHA)

Tie

Breastplate

Brass studs

Thigh plate

CHINESE COAT ARMOR (TONGXING DING JIA)

Shoulder defense (tongxing hubo)

Fabric backing

Embroidered dragon

Clasp

Riveted plate

Copper rivet (tongxing)

Arm defense (tongxing pizhuan)

11

Samurai warrior

THE PRESTIGIOUS STATUS OF the samurai, the warrior class of feudal Japan, was shown by their pair of swords—a long sword (katana) and a short sword (wakizashi). The swords were used chiefly for cutting, so armor had to permit free and rapid movement while also offering some protection against a blow. As a result, Japanese armor consisted of numerous plates of lacquered metal laced tightly together with colored silk. Early samurai armor comprised just a cuirass, sometimes worn with a helmet. The style and complexity of the armor evolved over the centuries until the whole body was protected, as in this modern armor (tosei gusoku) of the 19th century.

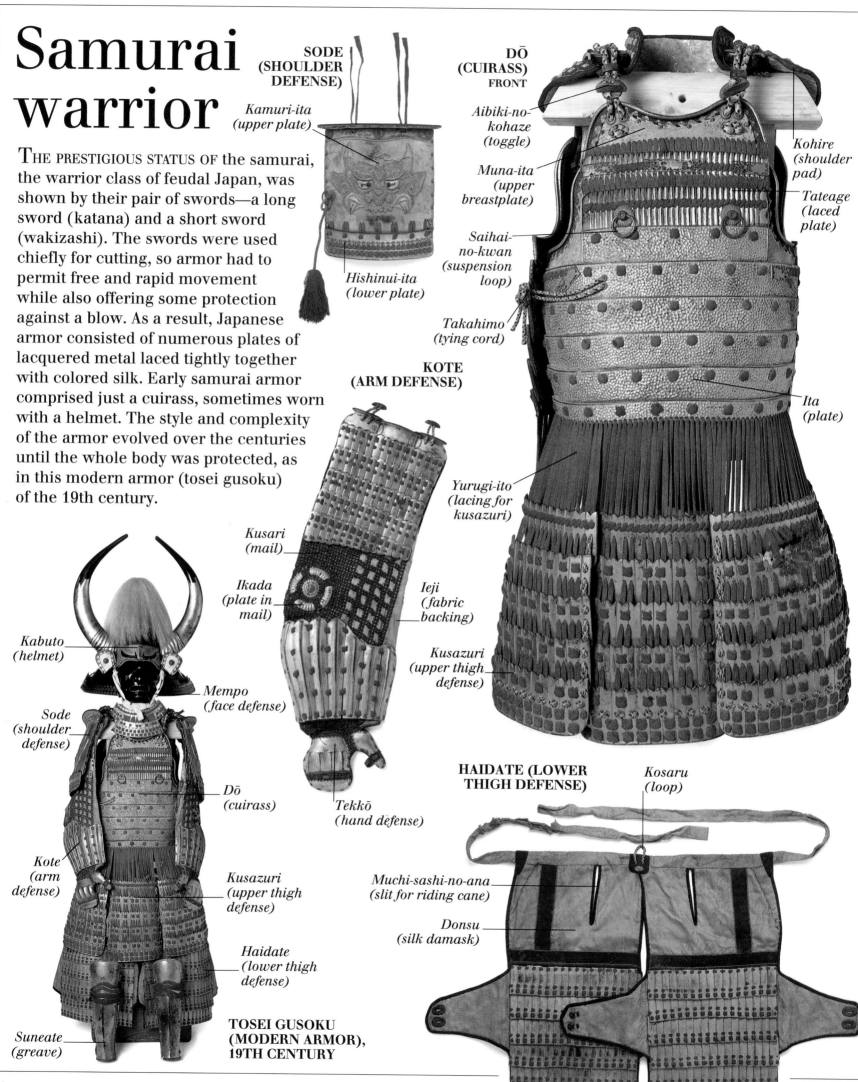

SODE (SHOULDER DEFENSE)

Kamuri-ita (upper plate)

Hishinui-ita (lower plate)

DŌ (CUIRASS) FRONT

Aibiki-no-kohaze (toggle)

Muna-ita (upper breastplate)

Saihai-no-kwan (suspension loop)

Takahimo (tying cord)

Kohire (shoulder pad)

Tateage (laced plate)

Ita (plate)

Yurugi-ito (lacing for kusazuri)

Kusazuri (upper thigh defense)

KOTE (ARM DEFENSE)

Kusari (mail)

Ikada (plate in mail)

Ieji (fabric backing)

Tekkō (hand defense)

Kabuto (helmet)

Mempo (face defense)

Sode (shoulder defense)

Dō (cuirass)

Kote (arm defense)

Kusazuri (upper thigh defense)

Haidate (lower thigh defense)

Suneate (greave)

TOSEI GUSOKU (MODERN ARMOR), 19TH CENTURY

HAIDATE (LOWER THIGH DEFENSE)

Kosaru (loop)

Muchi-sashi-no-ana (slit for riding cane)

Donsu (silk damask)

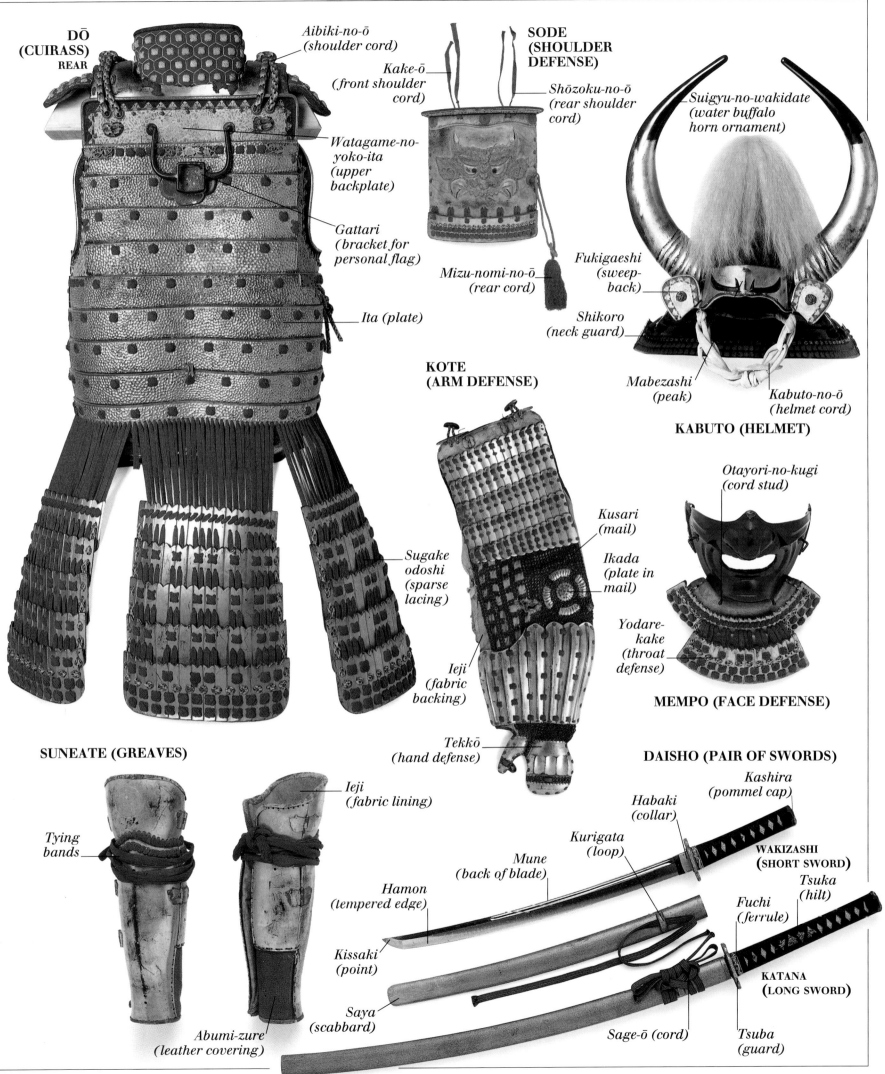

**DŌ
(CUIRASS)**
REAR

*Aibiki-no-ō
(shoulder cord)*

*Watagame-no-
yoko-ita
(upper
backplate)*

*Gattari
(bracket for
personal flag)*

Ita (plate)

*Sugake
odoshi
(sparse
lacing)*

**SODE
(SHOULDER
DEFENSE)**

*Kake-ō
(front shoulder
cord)*

*Shōzoku-no-ō
(rear shoulder
cord)*

*Mizu-nomi-no-ō
(rear cord)*

**KOTE
(ARM DEFENSE)**

*Kusari
(mail)*

*Ikada
(plate in
mail)*

*Ieji
(fabric
backing)*

*Tekkō
(hand defense)*

*Suigyu-no-wakidate
(water buffalo
horn ornament)*

*Fukigaeshi
(sweep-
back)*

*Shikoro
(neck guard)*

*Mabezashi
(peak)*

*Kabuto-no-ō
(helmet cord)*

KABUTO (HELMET)

*Otayori-no-kugi
(cord stud)*

*Yodare-
kake
(throat
defense)*

MEMPO (FACE DEFENSE)

SUNEATE (GREAVES)

*Ieji
(fabric lining)*

*Tying
bands*

*Abumi-zure
(leather covering)*

DAISHO (PAIR OF SWORDS)

*Kashira
(pommel cap)*

*Habaki
(collar)*

*Kurigata
(loop)*

*Mune
(back of blade)*

*Hamon
(tempered edge)*

*Kissaki
(point)*

*Saya
(scabbard)*

**WAKIZASHI
(SHORT SWORD)**

*Tsuka
(hilt)*

*Fuchi
(ferrule)*

**KATANA
(LONG SWORD)**

Sage-ō (cord)

*Tsuba
(guard)*

13

Ceremonial dress

SPECIAL CEREMONIAL UNIFORMS ARE A CHARACTERISTIC feature of military dress around the world. Such uniforms are typically more elaborate than those worn in battle and their designs are often based on the military clothing of earlier periods or on national costume. The elaborate dress of the early 19th-century Chinese court official was designed specifically for court functions, but it incorporated elements of practical armor in the form of studs and plates on the coat. The ceremonial uniform worn by a Napoleonic French general was distinguished by the lavish gold decoration on the coat and the tricolor plume in the cocked hat. Both the British uniforms shown here retain elements that survive from the military dress of earlier periods. The 12th Royal Lancers' czapska, for example, was the traditional headwear for lancers of many nations from the 18th century onward. The Greek Evzones, who guard the Presidential Palace and the Tomb of the Unknown Soldier in Athens, wear a distinctive uniform based on the Greek national costume. Members of the Pope's Swiss Guard at the Vatican wear a uniform that is very similar to that worn by their 16th-century predecessors.

BRITISH STAR OF THE ORDER OF THE BATH

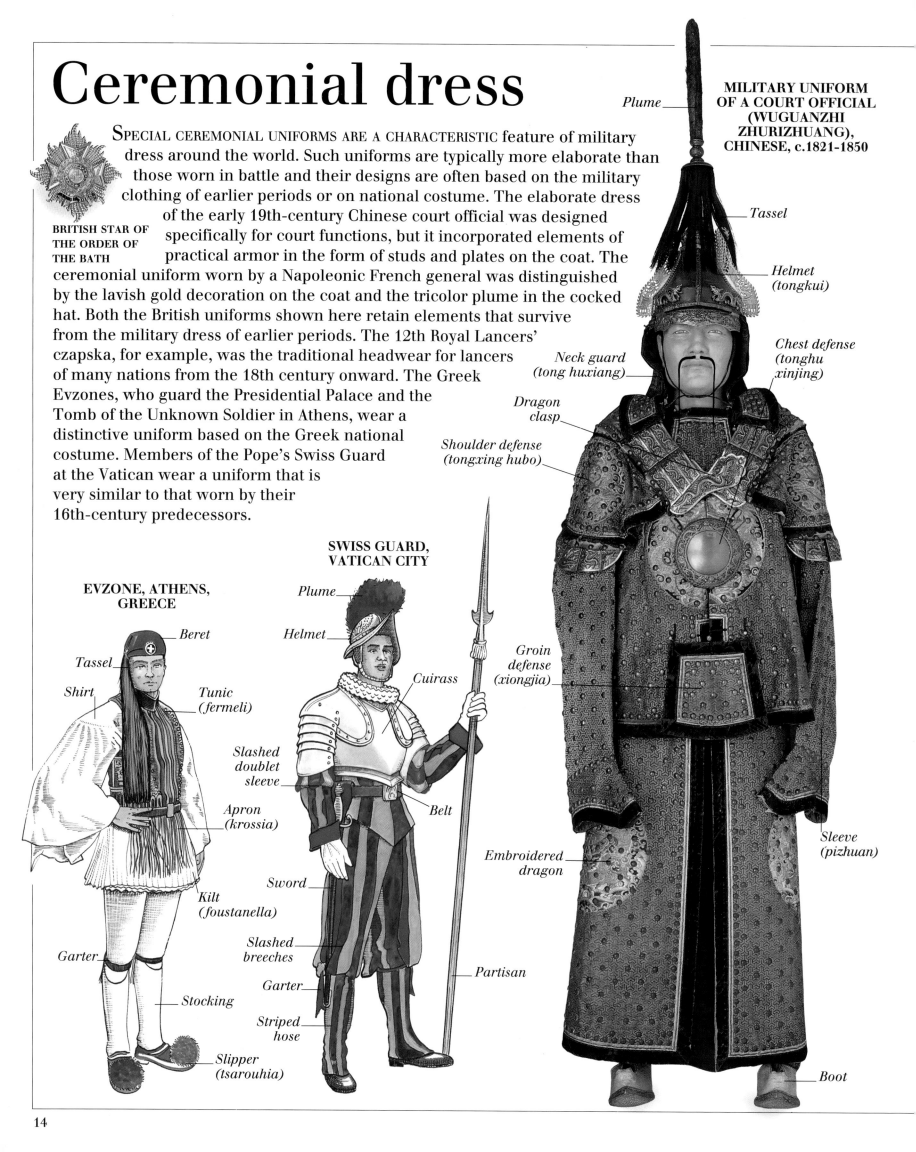

Plume

Tassel

Helmet (tongkui)

Neck guard (tong huxiang)

Chest defense (tonghu xinjing)

Dragon clasp

Shoulder defense (tongxing hubo)

Groin defense (xiongjia)

Sleeve (pizhuan)

Embroidered dragon

Boot

EVZONE, ATHENS, GREECE

Beret

Tassel

Shirt

Tunic (fermeli)

Apron (krossia)

Kilt (foustanella)

Garter

Stocking

Slipper (tsarouhia)

SWISS GUARD, VATICAN CITY

Plume

Helmet

Cuirass

Slashed doublet sleeve

Belt

Sword

Slashed breeches

Garter

Striped hose

Partisan

**OFFICER'S FULL DRESS COAT,
12TH ROYAL LANCERS, BRITISH
ARMY, c.1910**

Button

Silk tab

Shoulder strap
with rank insignia

Strap
loop

Quilted silk
lining

Piping

Skirt

Flat button

Gold lace

**OFFICER'S CZAPSKA,
12TH ROYAL LANCERS,
BRITISH ARMY, c.1910**

Orris cord

Cloth top

Gilt
plume
holder

Papier-
mâché
skull

Plume
socket

Tang of
plume

Lion's
head boss

Battle
honors

Swan
feathers

Royal
arms

Purl
embroidery

Chin
chain

Tricolor
plume

**GENERAL'S HAT, DRESS
UNIFORM, FRENCH
ARMY, c.1808-1812**

Gold lace

Cockade

Button

**FLAG OFFICER'S CEREMONIAL DAY COAT,
BRITAIN'S ROYAL NAVY, 1959-PRESENT**

Button

White collar

Gold lace

Shoulder strap
with rank insignia

Aiguillette

Sash of the Order
of the Garter

Decorations
and medals

Star of the Order
of the Garter

Star of the Order
of the Bath

Stripes for admiral
of the fleet

Badge of the
Order of the
Garter

Black
silk lining

Coat-tail

**GENERAL'S COAT, DRESS
UNIFORM, FRENCH
ARMY, c.1808-1812**

Gold oak-leaf
embroidery

Epaulet

Bavarian
Order of
Maximilian

Cuff

Turnback

Coat-
tail

Harquebusiers and pikemen

ARMIES IN THE 17TH CENTURY WERE LARGELY made up of lightly-armored mounted harquebusiers and infantry consisting of pikemen and musketeers. The harquebusier's armor included a three-bar pot helmet, a breastplate, a backplate, and sometimes an elbow gauntlet. His protective leather buff coat could be worn either under or instead of the body armor, and a gorget was occasionally worn by officers. The pikemen fought in close combat, defending the unarmored musketeers as they loaded their weapons. The pikemen wore a steel pot helmet, a backplate, a breastplate with tassets attached to cover the thighs, and a gorget to protect the throat. The sergeant of pikes carried a halberd instead of a pike as a sign of rank. The basic dress of the musketeer resembled civilian wear, although each member of a regiment usually wore a soldier's coat of the same color. The uniforms shown here are representative of those worn during the English Civil War (1642-1651). The two sides, Royalists and Parliamentarians, recognized each other on the battlefield by the color of their sashes, usually red for Royalists and orange for Parliamentarians.

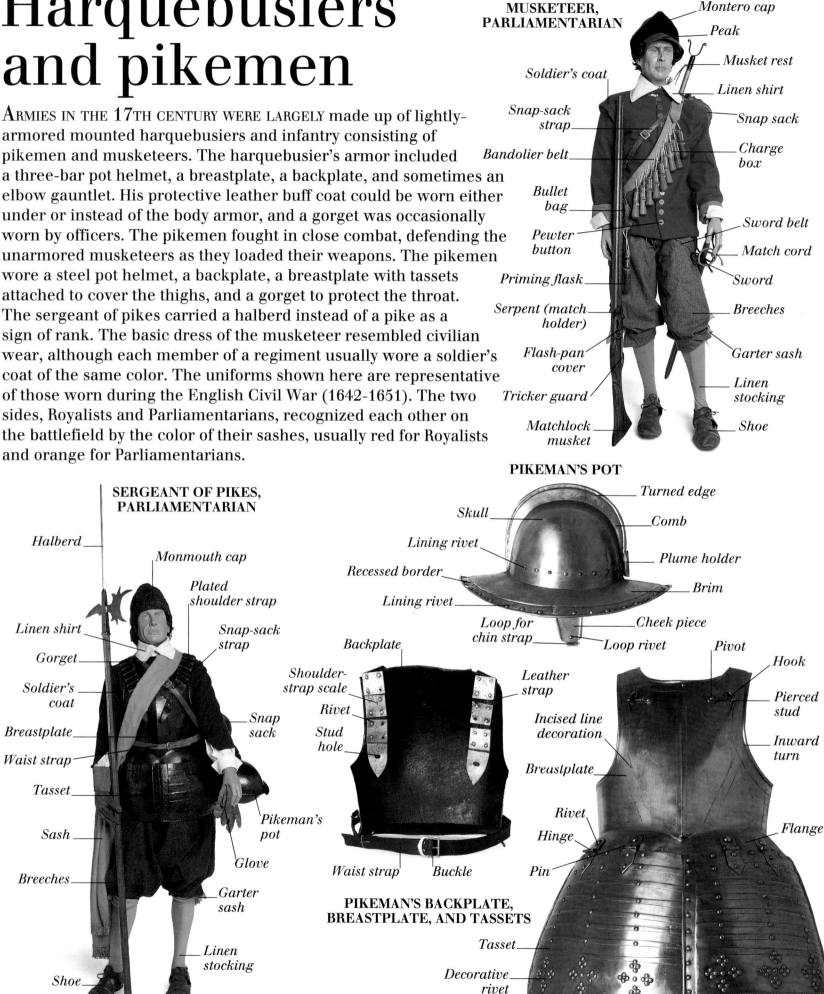

MUSKETEER, PARLIAMENTARIAN

Montero cap
Peak
Musket rest
Soldier's coat
Linen shirt
Snap-sack strap
Snap sack
Bandolier belt
Charge box
Bullet bag
Sword belt
Pewter button
Match cord
Priming flask
Sword
Serpent (match holder)
Breeches
Flash-pan cover
Garter sash
Tricker guard
Linen stocking
Matchlock musket
Shoe

SERGEANT OF PIKES, PARLIAMENTARIAN

Halberd
Monmouth cap
Plated shoulder strap
Linen shirt
Snap-sack strap
Gorget
Soldier's coat
Snap sack
Breastplate
Waist strap
Tasset
Sash
Pikeman's pot
Breeches
Glove
Garter sash
Linen stocking
Shoe

PIKEMAN'S POT

Turned edge
Skull
Comb
Lining rivet
Plume holder
Recessed border
Brim
Lining rivet
Loop for chin strap
Cheek piece
Loop rivet

PIKEMAN'S BACKPLATE, BREASTPLATE, AND TASSETS

Backplate
Shoulder-strap scale
Leather strap
Rivet
Stud hole
Incised line decoration
Breastplate
Pivot
Hook
Pierced stud
Inward turn
Rivet
Hinge
Flange
Pin
Waist strap
Buckle
Tasset
Decorative rivet

HARQUEBUSIER'S THREE-BAR POT

Peak

Faceguard

Rivet

Cheek piece

Hinge

Comb

Pivoting rivet

Skull

Simulated lame

Solid neck guard

HARQUEBUSIER'S BUFF COAT

Sleeve

Collar

Lace

Raised neck

Leather shoulder strap

Keyhole slot

Backplate

Mushroom-headed stud

Breastplate

Buckle

Leather waist strap

Flange

HARQUEBUSIER'S BACKPLATE AND BREASTPLATE

Cuff

HARQUEBUSIER'S ELBOW GAUNTLET

Laminated hand

Lining rivet

OFFICER OF HORSE (HARQUEBUSIER), ROYALIST

Felt hat

Plume

Black ribbon

Neckerchief

Gorget

Sword baldric

Sash

Carbine

Buff coat

Cassack

Bucket-top boot

Spur

Square toe

Carbine belt

Lace

Chamois leather inner sleeve

Gauntlet

Sword

Breeches

Butterfly spur leather

GORGET

Back

Gilt band

Mushroom-headed rivet

Keyhole slot

Front

Shoulder wing

Pewter button

Cuff

Collar

LINEN SHIRT

Wrist band

Linen toggle button

Cape panel

Front panel

Back panel

HARQUEBUSIER'S CASSACK

Headgear

**FRENCH KEPI,
19TH CENTURY**

Military headgear has had two main functions: to defend its wearer from enemies and the weather, and to make the wearer appear more impressive by increasing height and adding splendor. Helmets are designed to protect the skull. Some, such as the 1st-century AD Roman helmet, also shield the neck and cheeks. The Indo-Persian helmet (kulah khud) has a metal nose guard and a mail curtain (aventail) to protect the eyes and neck. Helmets and other types of military headgear have often been embellished with plumes, crests, national badges, and other symbols. Some types of headgear were part of a borrowed military tradition. The French Napoleonic lancer's square-topped cap (czapska), for example, was an exaggerated version of the headgear of earlier Polish horsemen. Civilian hat styles, such as the beret, have been widely adapted for military use by the addition of plumes, cap badges, and insignia. During the course of this century, armies around the world have adopted purely functional combat helmets, such as the net-covered steel helmet worn by U.S. troops in the Second World War.

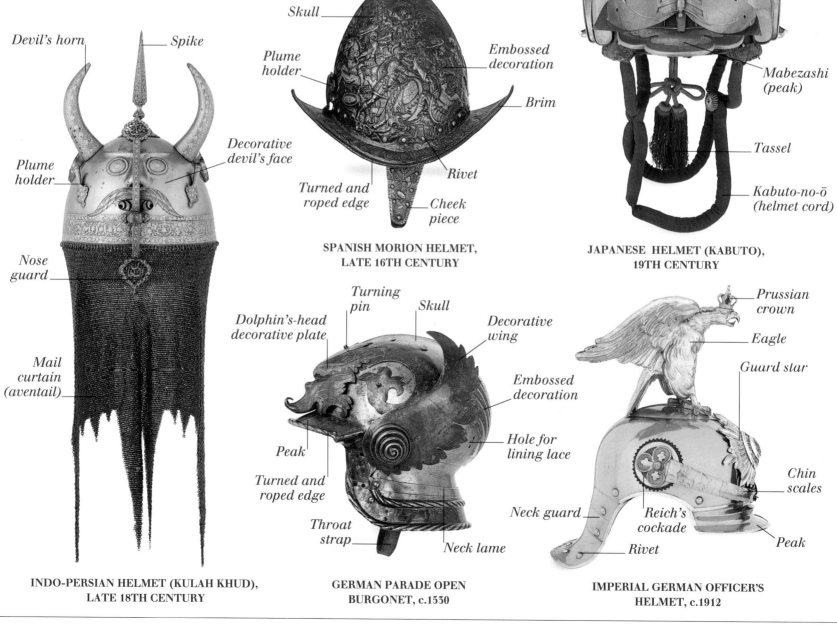

Crest knob

Plume holder

Brow band

Neck flange

Cheek piece

Tie

**ROMAN BRONZE
HELMET, 1ST CENTURY AD**

Fukigaeshi (sweepback)

Butterfly crest

Mabezashi (peak)

Tassel

Kabuto-no-ō (helmet cord)

**JAPANESE HELMET (KABUTO),
19TH CENTURY**

Devil's horn

Spike

Plume holder

Decorative devil's face

Plume holder

Nose guard

Mail curtain (aventail)

**INDO-PERSIAN HELMET (KULAH KHUD),
LATE 18TH CENTURY**

Skull

Plume holder

Embossed decoration

Brim

Turned and roped edge

Rivet

Cheek piece

**SPANISH MORION HELMET,
LATE 16TH CENTURY**

Turning pin

Skull

Dolphin's-head decorative plate

Decorative wing

Embossed decoration

Hole for lining lace

Peak

Turned and roped edge

Throat strap

Neck lame

**GERMAN PARADE OPEN
BURGONET, c.1530**

Prussian crown

Eagle

Guard star

Chin scales

Neck guard

Reich's cockade

Rivet

Peak

**IMPERIAL GERMAN OFFICER'S
HELMET, c.1912**

BRITISH CAVALRY BELL-TOP SHAKO, c.1830

- Horsehair plume
- Plume holder
- Crown
- Silver oak-leaf lace
- Chin scales
- Maltese-cross cap plate
- Chin strap
- Tassel
- Festoon

FRENCH DRAGOON OFFICER'S HELMET, c.1816-1825

- Plume
- Crest
- Skull
- Plume holder
- Chin scales
- Leopard-skin turban

FRENCH LANCER OFFICER'S CZAPSKA, c.1811-1815

- Plume
- Cloth top
- Cockade
- Cap plate
- Chin strap
- Flounder
- Napoleonic emblem
- Tassel

UNION OFFICER'S DRESS BICORN HAT, AMERICAN CIVIL WAR (1861-1865)

- Plume
- Union eagle
- Cockade
- Ribbon
- Tassel

UNION OFFICER'S SLOUCH HAT, AMERICAN CIVIL WAR (1861-1865)

- Rank badge
- Star
- Wreath
- Gold acorn

AUSTRIAN KAISERJÄGER OFFICER'S HAT, c.1914

- Ostrich feather
- Hunting horn
- Imperial eagle
- Brim
- Hat cord

BRITAIN'S ROYAL NAVY SENNET HAT, c.1910

- Plaited straw crown
- Ribbon binding
- Hat ribbon
- Brim
- Bow
- Ship's name
- Chin stay

U.S. STEEL HELMET, SECOND WORLD WAR (1939-1945)

- Steel helmet
- Net
- Band
- Strap

BRITISH ROYAL TANK REGIMENT OFFICER'S DRESS BERET AND HACKLE, c.1970

- First World War tank emblem
- Hackle
- Astrakhan beret
- Crown
- Wreath
- Gold braid band

BRITAIN'S WOMEN'S ROYAL NAVAL SERVICE OFFICER'S TRICORN HAT, 1956-PRESENT

- St. Edward's crown
- Detachable cover
- Ribbon
- Upturned brim
- Laurel-leaf wreath
- Anchor

USSR ARMORED UNIT OFFICER'S CAP, 1990

- Oak leaves
- Piping
- Hammer and Sickle symbol
- Cap band
- Red Star
- Cap cord

The American Revolution

From 1775 to 1783, the 13 British colonies on the eastern seaboard of North America fought successfully for independence. During this war the rebellious colonies formed the Continental Army and were aided by the French. Most infantrymen wore a similar style of long-tailed coat, although in different colors. Generally, the Americans wore blue, the British red (and so they became known as the redcoats), and the French white. Cocked hats were the usual headwear, although British grenadiers wore bearskins. Uniforms became simpler during the course of the war; for instance, some British units adopted short jackets.

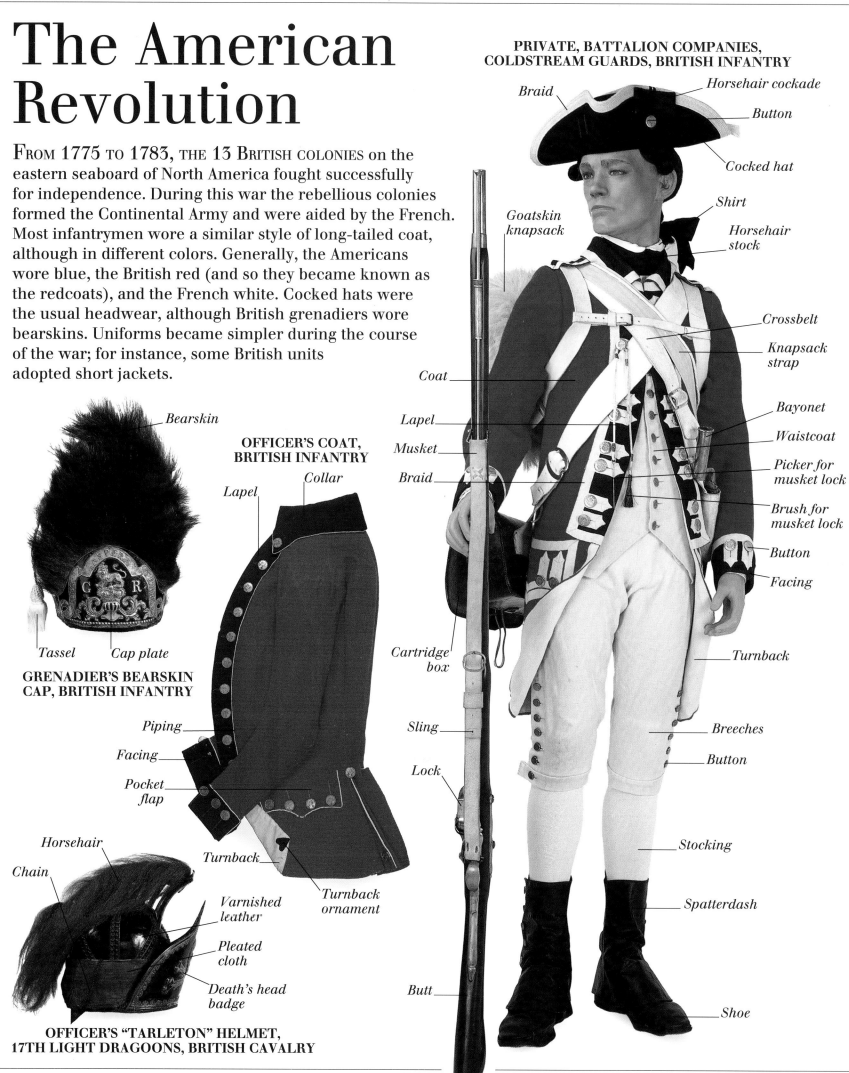

PRIVATE, BATTALION COMPANIES, COLDSTREAM GUARDS, BRITISH INFANTRY

Braid

Horsehair cockade

Button

Cocked hat

Goatskin knapsack

Shirt

Horsehair stock

Crossbelt

Knapsack strap

Coat

Bayonet

Lapel

Waistcoat

Musket

Picker for musket lock

Braid

Brush for musket lock

Button

Facing

Cartridge box

Turnback

Sling

Breeches

Lock

Button

Stocking

Spatterdash

Butt

Shoe

Bearskin

OFFICER'S COAT, BRITISH INFANTRY

Collar

Lapel

Tassel

Cap plate

GRENADIER'S BEARSKIN CAP, BRITISH INFANTRY

Piping

Facing

Pocket flap

Turnback

Turnback ornament

Horsehair

Chain

Varnished leather

Pleated cloth

Death's head badge

OFFICER'S "TARLETON" HELMET, 17TH LIGHT DRAGOONS, BRITISH CAVALRY

20

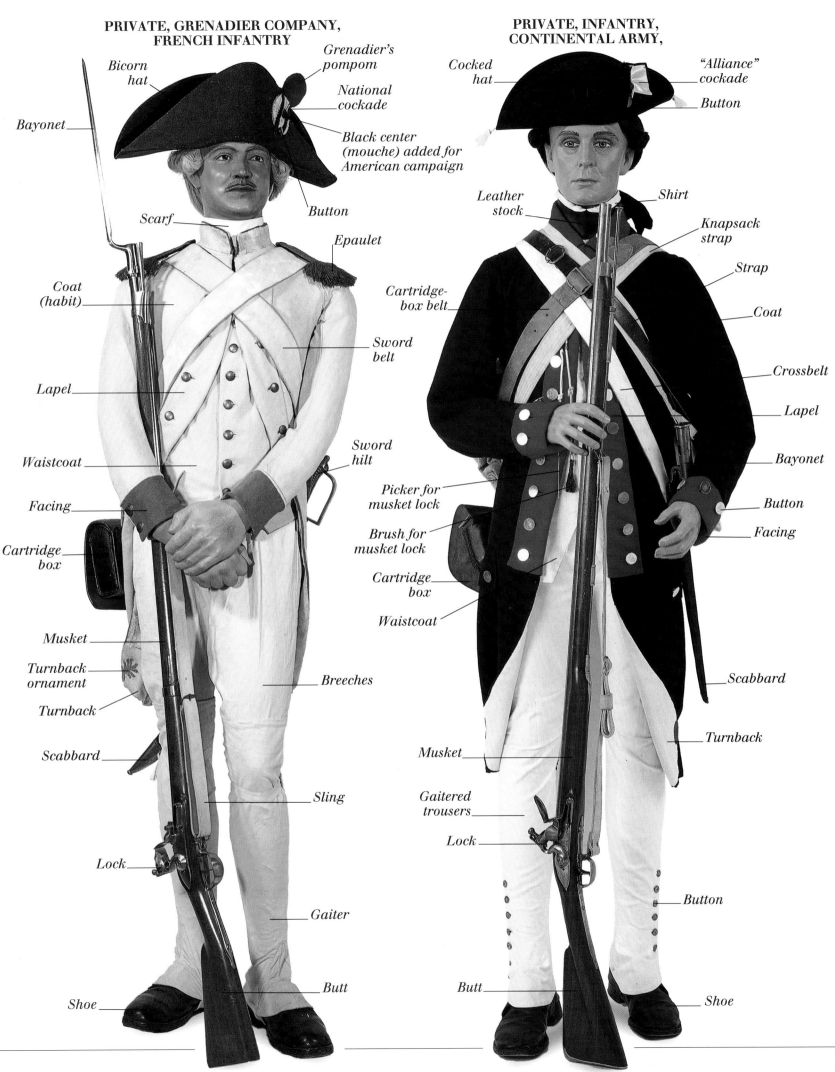

PRIVATE, GRENADIER COMPANY, FRENCH INFANTRY

Bicorn hat

Grenadier's pompom

National cockade

Black center (mouche) added for American campaign

Bayonet

Scarf

Button

Epaulet

Coat (habit)

Sword belt

Lapel

Waistcoat

Sword hilt

Facing

Cartridge box

Musket

Turnback ornament

Breeches

Turnback

Scabbard

Sling

Lock

Gaiter

Shoe

Butt

PRIVATE, INFANTRY, CONTINENTAL ARMY,

Cocked hat

"Alliance" cockade

Button

Leather stock

Shirt

Knapsack strap

Strap

Cartridge-box belt

Coat

Crossbelt

Lapel

Bayonet

Picker for musket lock

Button

Brush for musket lock

Facing

Cartridge box

Waistcoat

Scabbard

Turnback

Musket

Gaitered trousers

Lock

Button

Butt

Shoe

Hussars and carabiniers

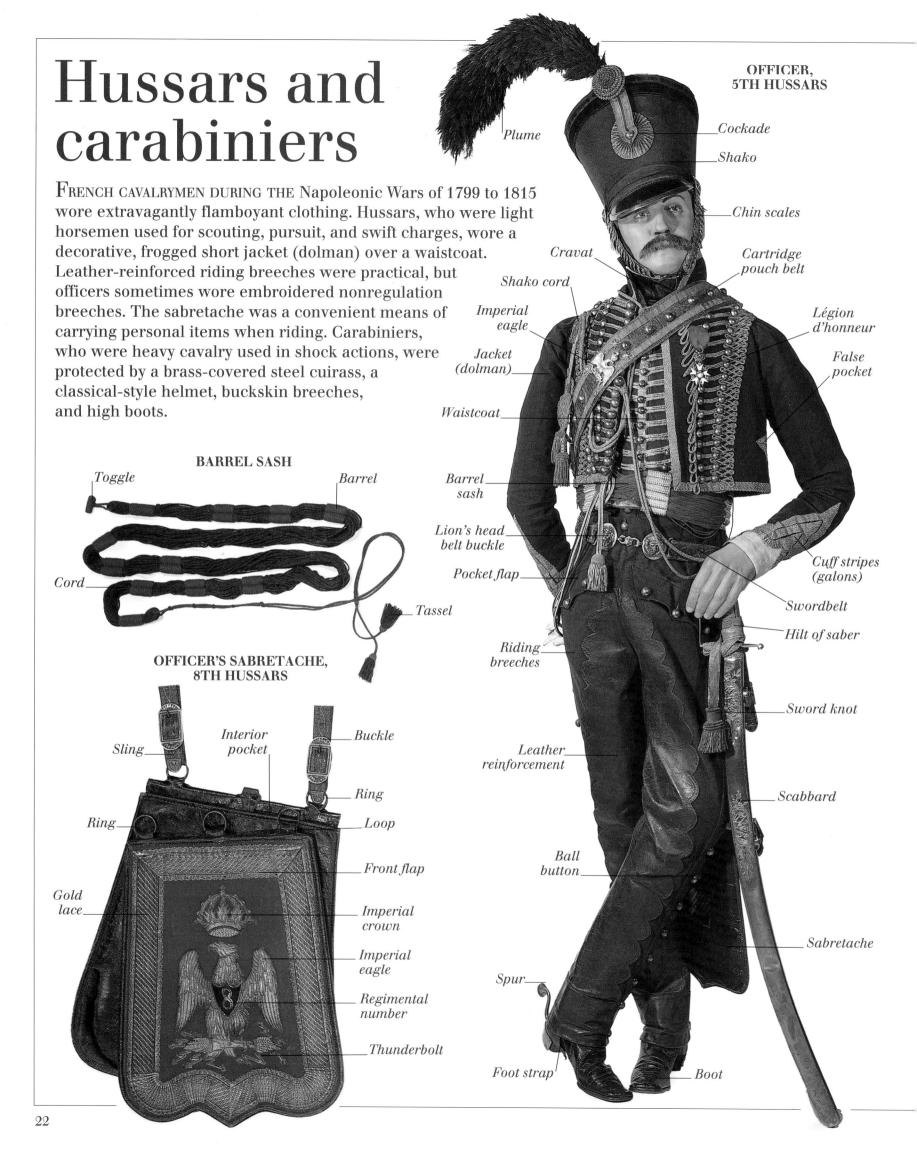

FRENCH CAVALRYMEN DURING THE Napoleonic Wars of 1799 to 1815 wore extravagantly flamboyant clothing. Hussars, who were light horsemen used for scouting, pursuit, and swift charges, wore a decorative, frogged short jacket (dolman) over a waistcoat. Leather-reinforced riding breeches were practical, but officers sometimes wore embroidered nonregulation breeches. The sabretache was a convenient means of carrying personal items when riding. Carabiniers, who were heavy cavalry used in shock actions, were protected by a brass-covered steel cuirass, a classical-style helmet, buckskin breeches, and high boots.

OFFICER, 5TH HUSSARS

Plume
Cockade
Shako
Chin scales
Cravat
Cartridge pouch belt
Shako cord
Imperial eagle
Légion d'honneur
Jacket (dolman)
False pocket
Waistcoat
Barrel sash
Lion's head belt buckle
Pocket flap
Cuff stripes (galons)
Swordbelt
Hilt of saber
Riding breeches
Sword knot
Leather reinforcement
Scabbard
Ball button
Sabretache
Spur
Foot strap
Boot

BARREL SASH

Toggle
Barrel
Cord
Tassel

OFFICER'S SABRETACHE, 8TH HUSSARS

Sling
Interior pocket
Buckle
Ring
Ring
Loop
Front flap
Gold lace
Imperial crown
Imperial eagle
Regimental number
Thunderbolt

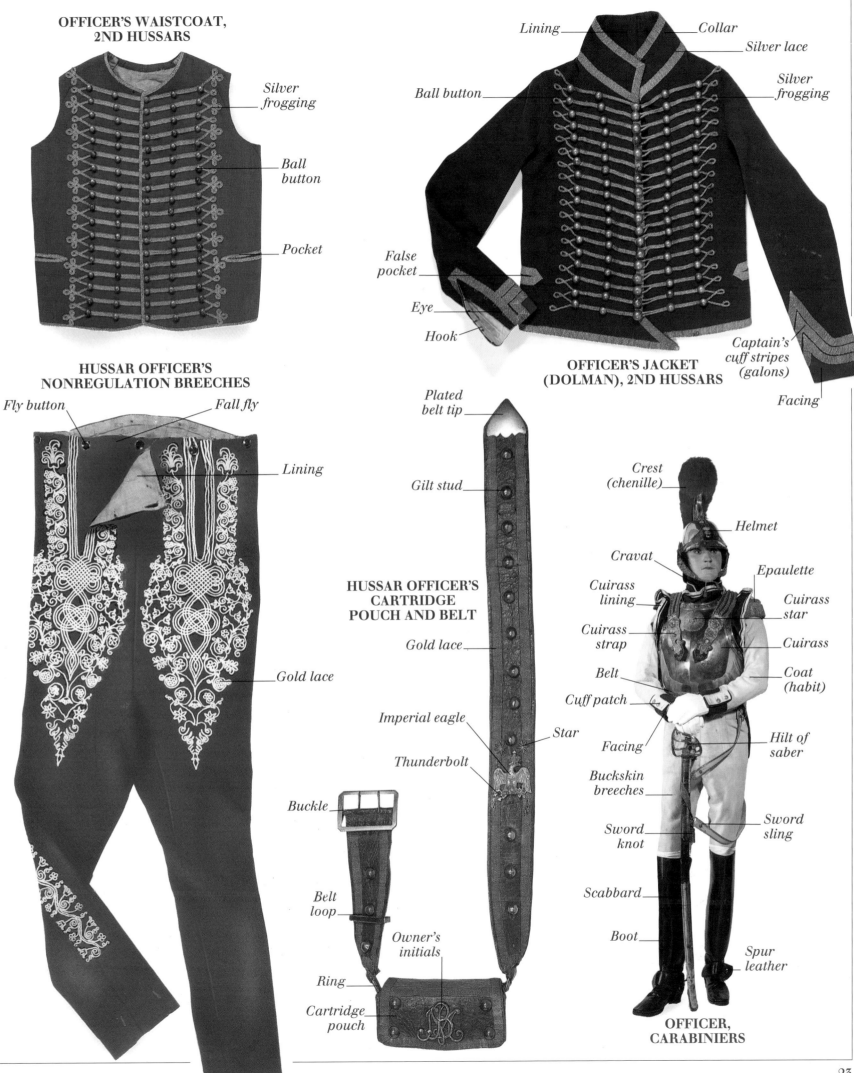

OFFICER'S WAISTCOAT, 2ND HUSSARS

Silver frogging

Ball button

Pocket

OFFICER'S JACKET (DOLMAN), 2ND HUSSARS

Lining

Collar

Silver lace

Ball button

Silver frogging

False pocket

Eye

Hook

Captain's cuff stripes (galons)

Facing

HUSSAR OFFICER'S NONREGULATION BREECHES

Fly button

Fall fly

Lining

Gold lace

HUSSAR OFFICER'S CARTRIDGE POUCH AND BELT

Plated belt tip

Gilt stud

Gold lace

Imperial eagle

Star

Thunderbolt

Buckle

Belt loop

Ring

Cartridge pouch

Owner's initials

OFFICER, CARABINIERS

Crest (chenille)

Helmet

Cravat

Epaulette

Cuirass lining

Cuirass star

Cuirass strap

Cuirass

Belt

Coat (habit)

Cuff patch

Facing

Hilt of saber

Buckskin breeches

Sword sling

Sword knot

Scabbard

Boot

Spur leather

Grenadiers and fusiliers

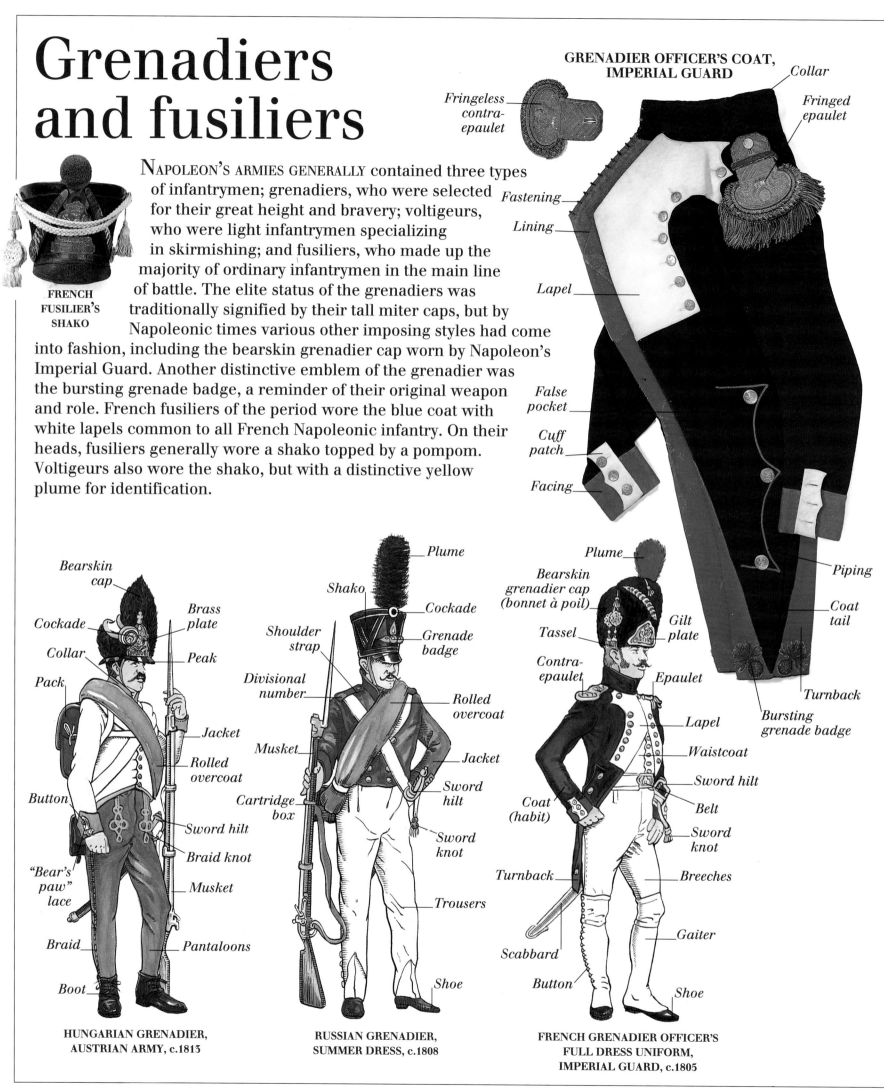

GRENADIER OFFICER'S COAT, IMPERIAL GUARD

NAPOLEON'S ARMIES GENERALLY contained three types of infantrymen; grenadiers, who were selected for their great height and bravery; voltigeurs, who were light infantrymen specializing in skirmishing; and fusiliers, who made up the majority of ordinary infantrymen in the main line of battle. The elite status of the grenadiers was traditionally signified by their tall miter caps, but by Napoleonic times various other imposing styles had come into fashion, including the bearskin grenadier cap worn by Napoleon's Imperial Guard. Another distinctive emblem of the grenadier was the bursting grenade badge, a reminder of their original weapon and role. French fusiliers of the period wore the blue coat with white lapels common to all French Napoleonic infantry. On their heads, fusiliers generally wore a shako topped by a pompom. Voltigeurs also wore the shako, but with a distinctive yellow plume for identification.

FRENCH FUSILIER'S SHAKO

Fringeless contra-epaulet

Collar

Fringed epaulet

Fastening

Lining

Lapel

False pocket

Cuff patch

Facing

Piping

Coat tail

Turnback

Bursting grenade badge

Hungarian Grenadier labels:
Bearskin cap
Cockade
Collar
Pack
Button
"Bear's paw" lace
Braid
Boot
Brass plate
Peak
Jacket
Rolled overcoat
Sword hilt
Braid knot
Musket
Pantaloons

HUNGARIAN GRENADIER, AUSTRIAN ARMY, c.1813

Russian Grenadier labels:
Shako
Shoulder strap
Divisional number
Musket
Cartridge box
Plume
Cockade
Grenade badge
Rolled overcoat
Jacket
Sword hilt
Sword knot
Trousers
Shoe

RUSSIAN GRENADIER, SUMMER DRESS, c.1808

French Grenadier Officer labels:
Plume
Bearskin grenadier cap (bonnet à poil)
Tassel
Contra-epaulet
Coat (habit)
Turnback
Scabbard
Button
Gilt plate
Epaulet
Lapel
Waistcoat
Sword hilt
Belt
Sword knot
Breeches
Gaiter
Shoe

FRENCH GRENADIER OFFICER'S FULL DRESS UNIFORM, IMPERIAL GUARD, c.1805

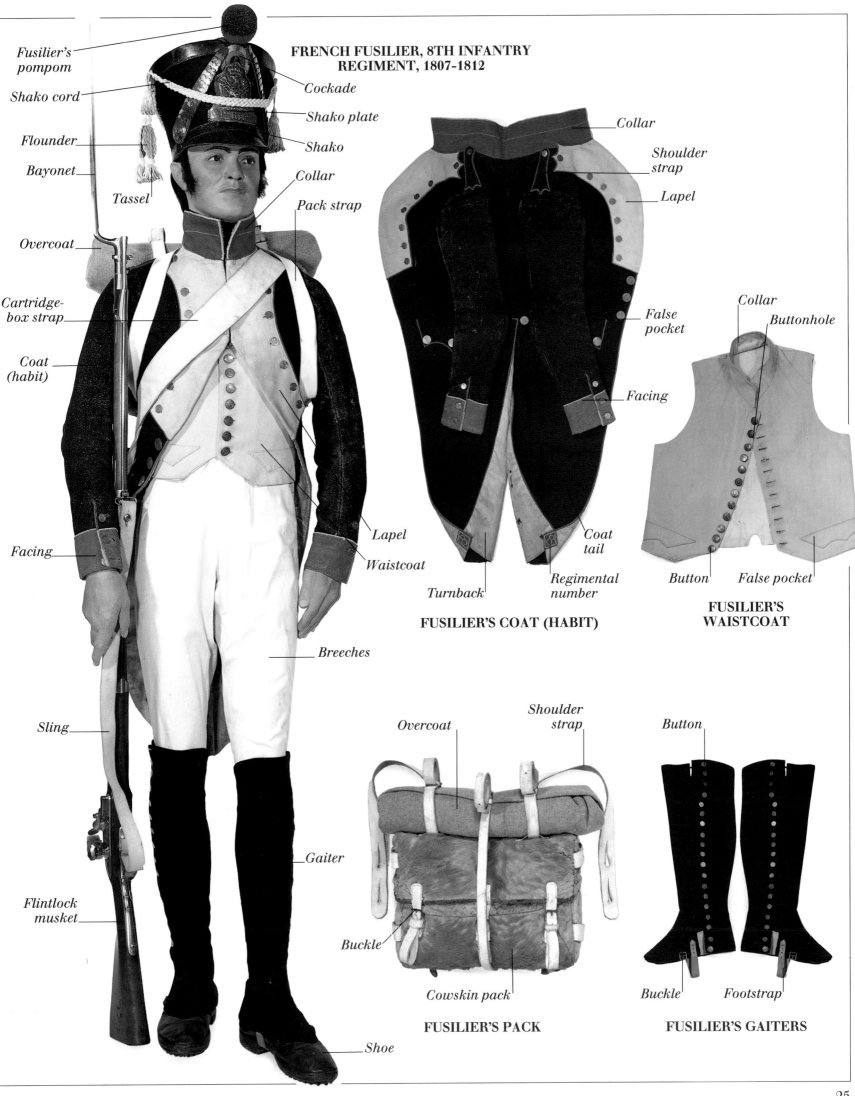

FRENCH FUSILIER, 8TH INFANTRY REGIMENT, 1807-1812

Fusilier's pompom

Shako cord

Flounder

Bayonet

Tassel

Overcoat

Cartridge-box strap

Coat (habit)

Facing

Sling

Flintlock musket

Cockade

Shako plate

Shako

Collar

Pack strap

Lapel

Waistcoat

Breeches

Gaiter

Shoe

Collar

Shoulder strap

Lapel

False pocket

Facing

Turnback

Regimental number

Coat tail

FUSILIER'S COAT (HABIT)

Collar

Buttonhole

Button

False pocket

FUSILIER'S WAISTCOAT

Overcoat

Shoulder strap

Buckle

Cowskin pack

FUSILIER'S PACK

Button

Buckle

Footstrap

FUSILIER'S GAITERS

25

Epaulets and insignia

ARMIES HAVE LONG USED EPAULETS AND INSIGNIA to show the wearer's rank, unit, branch of service, length of service, or a specialist qualification. Epaulets are most usually associated with officer rank, but they have been worn by other personnel to embellish uniforms, indicate elite status, or even to protect the shoulder against sword cuts. Originally, only one epaulet was worn. Then a fringeless epaulet for the other shoulder was introduced, called the contra-epaulet.

By the end of the 18th century, epaulets were usually fringed and worn in pairs. British stars and crowns, along with other badges of rank, have been worn on epaulets in solid metal, wire, appliqué, and embroidered forms. In the modern army, badges are often on a cloth "slide" which slips over a plain epaulet. All parts of the sleeve have been used for displaying insignia, including army and navy specialist badges or unit patches. The cap and collar are also used for displaying badges of rank and unit.

ITALIAN INFANTRY OFFICER'S CAP BADGE, FIRST WORLD WAR (1914-1918)

Fringe
Buttonhole

FRENCH FIELD OFFICER'S EPAULET, c.1770-1780

Contra-epaulet

Bursting grenade
Fringe
Epaulet

FRENCH CARABINIER CAPTAIN'S EPAULET AND CONTRA-EPAULET, c.1810-1815

Cloth strap

Woollen fringe

FRENCH INFANTRY SERGEANT'S EPAULETS, c.1805-1815

ARMY EPAULETS

BRITISH LORD LIEUTENANT'S EPAULETS, c.1840

Silver lace strap
Button
Embroidered edging
Crown
Crossed sword and baton
Silver crescent

Fastener
Strap
Silk pad
Bullions
Mold

Regimental initials of Scots Greys
Crescent
Thistle
Bursting grenade

BRITISH CAVALRY EPAULETS, c.1830-1840

BRITISH CAVALRY EPAULETS, c.1850

Trophy of Arms
Button
Fixed scale
Star of the Order of the Bath
Lace

Roped edging
Dull and bright gold bullions

Crescent
Button
Bursting grenade

BRITISH CAVALRY EPAULETS, c.1825

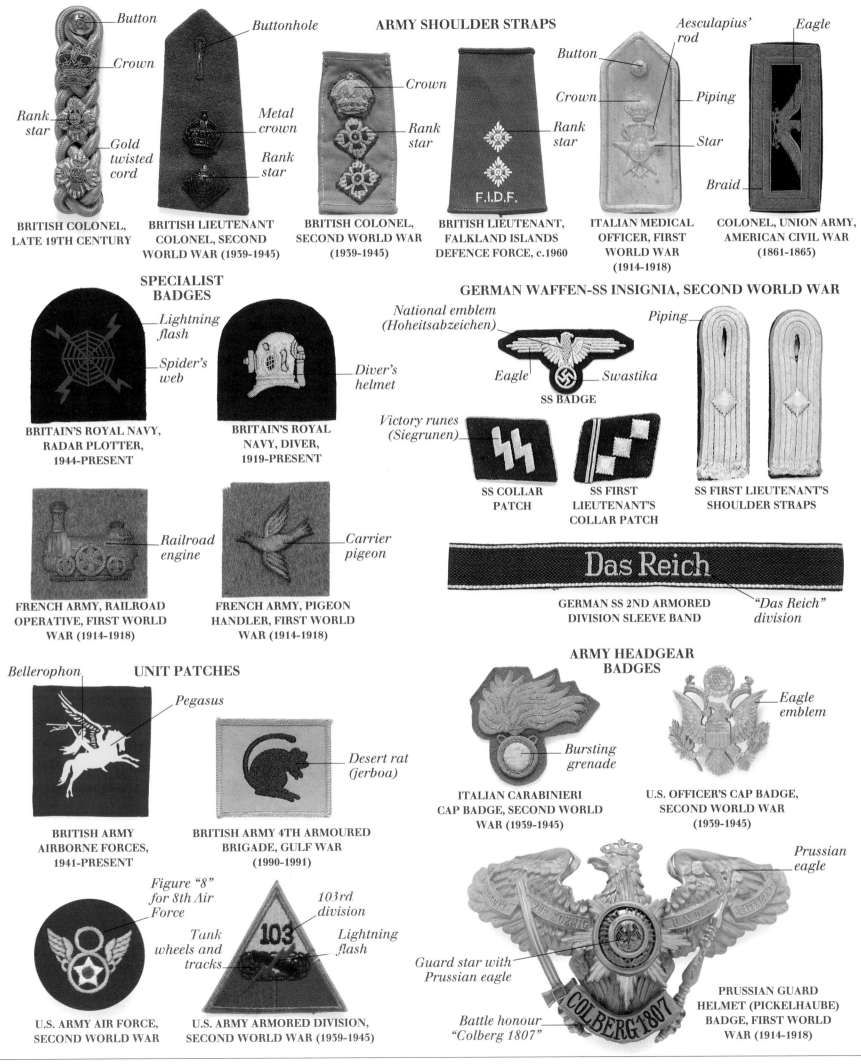

ARMY SHOULDER STRAPS

Button · **Crown** · **Rank star** · **Gold twisted cord**

BRITISH COLONEL, LATE 19TH CENTURY

Buttonhole · **Metal crown** · **Rank star**

BRITISH LIEUTENANT COLONEL, SECOND WORLD WAR (1939-1945)

Crown · **Rank star**

BRITISH COLONEL, SECOND WORLD WAR (1939-1945)

Rank star

F.I.D.F.

BRITISH LIEUTENANT, FALKLAND ISLANDS DEFENCE FORCE, c.1960

Aesculapius' rod · **Button** · **Crown** · **Piping** · **Star**

ITALIAN MEDICAL OFFICER, FIRST WORLD WAR (1914-1918)

Eagle · **Braid**

COLONEL, UNION ARMY, AMERICAN CIVIL WAR (1861-1865)

SPECIALIST BADGES

Lightning flash · **Spider's web**

BRITAIN'S ROYAL NAVY, RADAR PLOTTER, 1944-PRESENT

Diver's helmet

BRITAIN'S ROYAL NAVY, DIVER, 1919-PRESENT

Railroad engine

FRENCH ARMY, RAILROAD OPERATIVE, FIRST WORLD WAR (1914-1918)

Carrier pigeon

FRENCH ARMY, PIGEON HANDLER, FIRST WORLD WAR (1914-1918)

GERMAN WAFFEN-SS INSIGNIA, SECOND WORLD WAR

National emblem (Hoheitsabzeichen) · **Eagle** · **Swastika**

SS BADGE

Piping

Victory runes (Siegrunen)

SS COLLAR PATCH

SS FIRST LIEUTENANT'S COLLAR PATCH

SS FIRST LIEUTENANT'S SHOULDER STRAPS

Das Reich

GERMAN SS 2ND ARMORED DIVISION SLEEVE BAND · "Das Reich" division

UNIT PATCHES

Bellerophon · **Pegasus**

BRITISH ARMY AIRBORNE FORCES, 1941-PRESENT

Desert rat (jerboa)

BRITISH ARMY 4TH ARMOURED BRIGADE, GULF WAR (1990-1991)

Figure "8" for 8th Air Force

U.S. ARMY AIR FORCE, SECOND WORLD WAR

Tank wheels and tracks · **103rd division** · **Lightning flash**

103

U.S. ARMY ARMORED DIVISION, SECOND WORLD WAR (1939-1945)

ARMY HEADGEAR BADGES

Bursting grenade

ITALIAN CARABINIERI CAP BADGE, SECOND WORLD WAR (1939-1945)

Eagle emblem

U.S. OFFICER'S CAP BADGE, SECOND WORLD WAR (1939-1945)

Prussian eagle · **Guard star with Prussian eagle** · **Battle honour "Colberg 1807"**

COLBERG 1807

PRUSSIAN GUARD HELMET (PICKELHAUBE) BADGE, FIRST WORLD WAR (1914-1918)

Nelson's navy

HORATIO NELSON LED BRITAIN'S Royal Navy to victory over the French in the Battle of Trafalgar (1805), the decisive naval engagement of the Napoleonic Wars (1799-1815). Nelson's full dress coat is embellished with decorations earned during his distinguished career. This style of uniform was worn by all British vice-admirals from 1795 to 1812; it comprises a white linen shirt, waistcoat, breeches, a cocked hat, a coat edged with gold lace, and epaulets bearing two stars. The French navy of this period had a wide range of uniforms. Two examples intended for everyday wear are shown here. The yellow uniform worn by the Provisional Sailor's Battalion, who fought in the French colony of Île de France (now Mauritius), was of a practical design suitable for land warfare. The French lieutenant's undress uniform (a type of uniform designed for use in battle) had a navy blue coat buttoned over a white waistcoat; the white trousers and black hat were nonregulation wear.

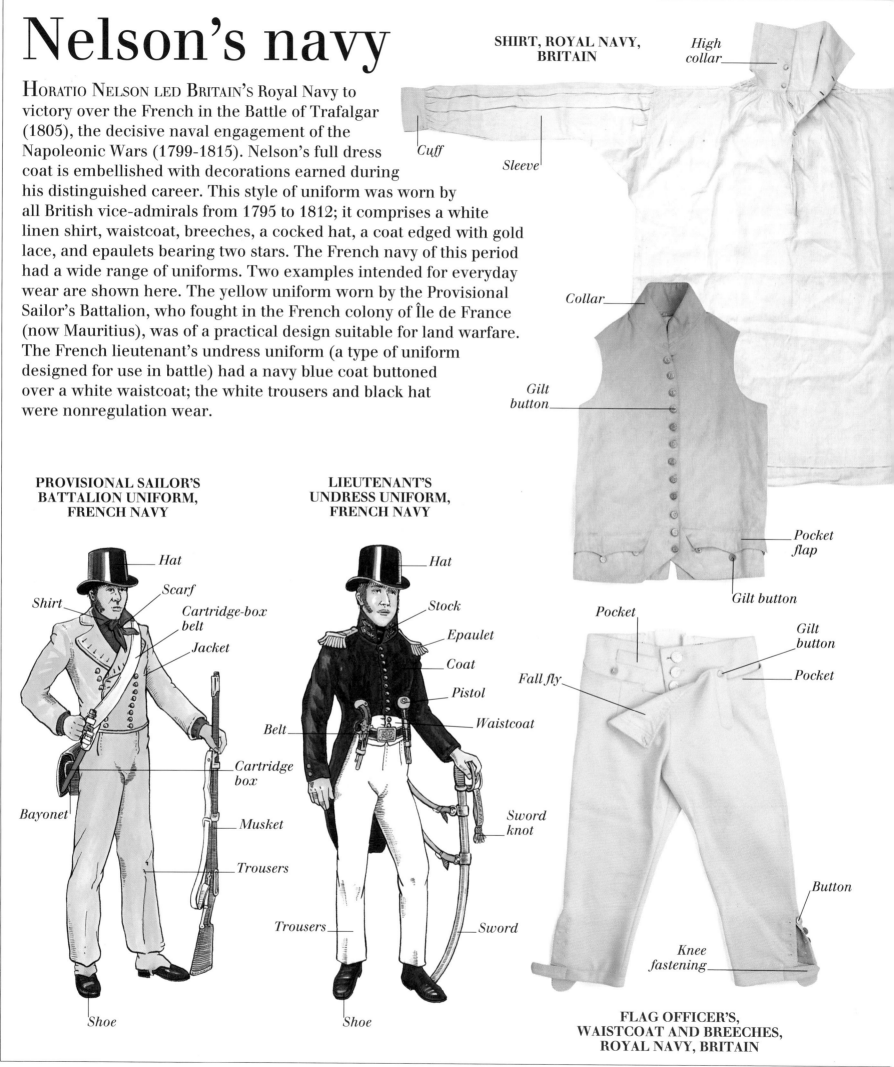

SHIRT, ROYAL NAVY, BRITAIN

High collar

Cuff

Sleeve

Collar

Gilt button

Pocket flap

Gilt button

PROVISIONAL SAILOR'S BATTALION UNIFORM, FRENCH NAVY

Hat

Scarf

Shirt

Cartridge-box belt

Jacket

Bayonet

Cartridge box

Musket

Trousers

Shoe

LIEUTENANT'S UNDRESS UNIFORM, FRENCH NAVY

Hat

Stock

Epaulet

Coat

Pistol

Belt

Waistcoat

Sword knot

Trousers

Sword

Shoe

Pocket

Fall fly

Gilt button

Pocket

Button

Knee fastening

FLAG OFFICER'S, WAISTCOAT AND BREECHES, ROYAL NAVY, BRITAIN

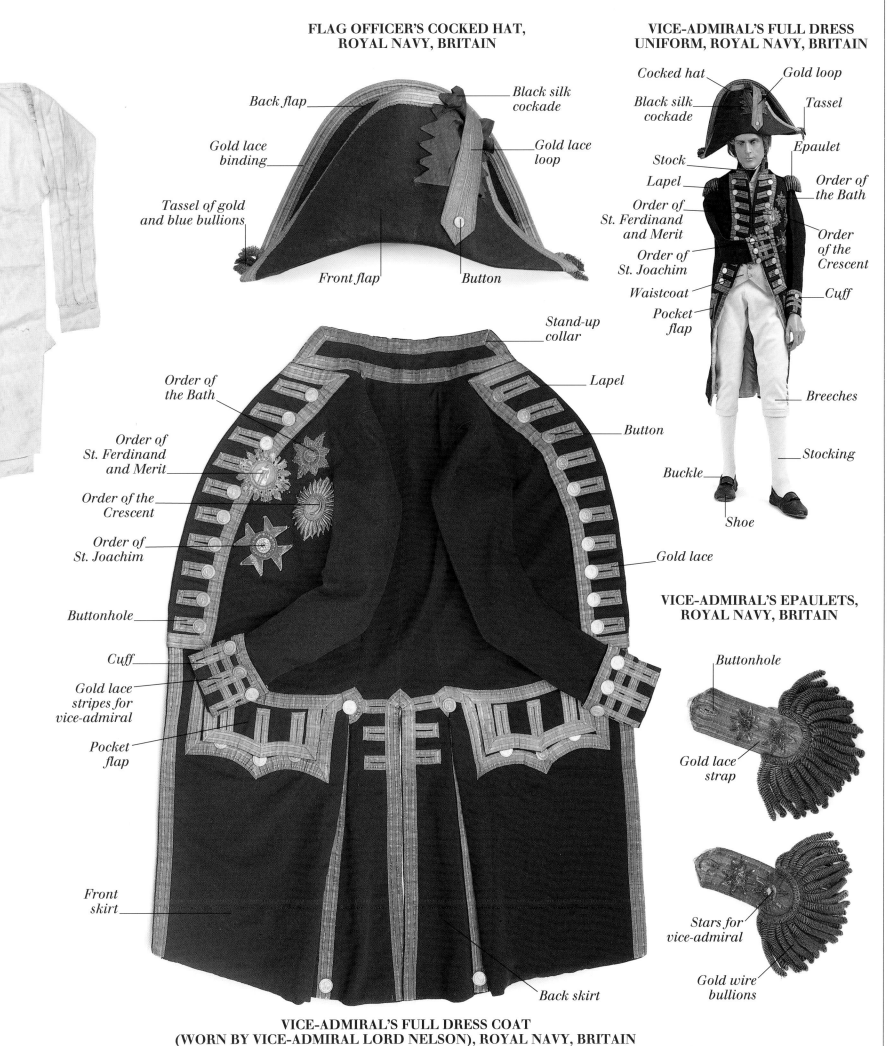

FLAG OFFICER'S COCKED HAT, ROYAL NAVY, BRITAIN

Back flap
Black silk cockade
Gold lace binding
Gold lace loop
Tassel of gold and blue bullions
Front flap
Button

VICE-ADMIRAL'S FULL DRESS UNIFORM, ROYAL NAVY, BRITAIN

Cocked hat
Gold loop
Black silk cockade
Tassel
Stock
Epaulet
Lapel
Order of the Bath
Order of St. Ferdinand and Merit
Order of the Crescent
Order of St. Joachim
Waistcoat
Cuff
Pocket flap
Breeches
Stocking
Buckle
Shoe

Stand-up collar
Order of the Bath
Lapel
Order of St. Ferdinand and Merit
Button
Order of the Crescent
Order of St. Joachim
Buttonhole
Gold lace
Cuff
Gold lace stripes for vice-admiral
Pocket flap
Front skirt
Back skirt

VICE-ADMIRAL'S EPAULETS, ROYAL NAVY, BRITAIN

Buttonhole
Gold lace strap
Stars for vice-admiral
Gold wire bullions

VICE-ADMIRAL'S FULL DRESS COAT (WORN BY VICE-ADMIRAL LORD NELSON), ROYAL NAVY, BRITAIN

Medals and orders

MOST NATIONS REALIZE THE IMPORTANCE of recognizing soldiers' achievements by rewarding bravery with visible signs of distinction. Some countries maintain orders of chivalry. Each order has various levels of honors, such as Members, Officers, Companions, or Knights. Some orders limit membership to certain groups. For instance, the French Order of St. Louis was only available to officers, but the French Légion d'Honneur has fewer restrictions. Gallantry awards cover many different activities, and the most prestigious reward acts of supreme valor, such as the U.S. Congressional Medal of Honor. Frequently, a soldier's service in a particular campaign is recognized by the award of a single medal, which may have additional named bars to show participation in specific battles or actions. For example, the British Queen's South Africa Medal shown here has bars for fighting in five actions or areas, including Johannesburg and Orange Free State. Full-size medals are usually worn only on ceremonial occasions; more commonly, ribbons alone are worn, and miniature medals are used on evening dress.

BRITISH SECOND ANGLO-AFGHAN WAR (1878-1880)

Ribbon bar for everyday wear

North Africa bar, 1942-1943

Full-size medals for ceremonial wear

1939-1945 Star

King's cipher

Africa Star

Defence Medal, 1939-1945

The War Medal, 1939-1945

King George VI

Miniature medals for evening wear

U.S. CONGRESSIONAL MEDAL OF HONOR (ARMY VERSION)

Eagle

Laurel-leaf wreath

Goddess Minerva

U.S. ARMY DISTINGUISHED SERVICE MEDAL

Eagle

U.S. PURPLE HEART FOR WOUNDS IN ACTION

Oak-leaf cluster

Washington family crest

George Washington

IMPERIAL RUSSIAN MILITARY ORDER OF ST. VLADIMIR, 4TH CLASS

USSR ORDER OF THE RED STAR

Figure holding a rifle

IMPERIAL RUSSIAN MILITARY ORDER OF ST. ANNE, 2ND CLASS

Enamel cross

St. Anne

Crossed swords

Enamel cross

Crossed swords

Imperial Russian mantle

Hammer and Sickle

FRENCH ROYAL MILITARY ORDER OF ST. LOUIS

Fleur-de-lys

Sword impaling a laurel wreath

BRITISH COMPANION OF THE ORDER OF THE INDIAN EMPIRE

Crown

Queen Victoria

Enamel rose

FRENCH CROIX DE GUERRE

Star

Palm

Pin

Crossed swords

Symbolic head of Marianne

FRENCH LÉGION D'HONNEUR, 5TH CLASS

Laurel-leaf wreath

Oak-leaf wreath

Symbolic head of Marianne

UNITED NATIONS' KOREA MEDAL (1950-1953)

Korean action bar

United Nations' symbol

BRITISH INDIA GENERAL SERVICE MEDAL

3rd Burma War bar

Victory

Seated warrior

BRITISH VICTORIA CROSS

Lion

Crown

BRITISH QUEEN'S SOUTH AFRICA MEDAL

Diamond Hill

Cape Colony

Belfast

Johannesburg

Orange Free State

Queen Victoria

GERMAN WILHELM ERNST WAR CROSS

Falcon

Crossed swords

Laurel-leaf wreath

PRUSSIAN IRON CROSS, 2ND CLASS

Crown

POLISH CROSS OF VALOR

Eagle

SPANISH MILITARY ORDER OF ST. HERMENEGILDO

Crown

St. Hermenegildo

FINNISH WAR MEDAL, SECOND WORLD WAR (1939-1945)

Figure holding a rifle

Arm holding a sword

Shield

EGYPTIAN WAR-WOUND MEDAL

Soldier

Wound stripe

OMAN GENERAL SERVICE MEDAL

Action bar (dhofar)

Curved dagger (khunjar)

Union forces

UNION FORCES DURING THE American Civil War (1861-1865) generally wore uniforms characterized by dark-blue coats, sky-blue trousers, and kepi-style forage caps. An officer's rank was shown by insignia on his epaulet straps; generals could also be identified by button grouping. The major-general's uniform, shown here, is distinguished by the two stars on the kepi and epaulet straps, the buttons grouped in threes, and the pale silk sash. A feature of cavalry dress was a short jacket edged with yellow piping. In winter, the infantry wore a dull-blue caped overcoat like that worn by the New York Volunteer infantryman shown here. The New York sergeant wore a frock coat with rank chevrons on the sleeves and a red worsted sash. Several volunteer units wore decorative zouave uniforms based on those originally worn by French forces in North Africa.

GENERAL'S KEPI

Braid wreath

Braid knotting

Rank star

Chin strap

GENERAL'S FROCK COAT

Collar

Epaulet strap

Rank star

Button

CARTRIDGE BOX

GENERAL'S SILK SASH

Tassel

GENERAL'S SWORD BELT

Gilt belt plate

Sword sling

Sling swivel for sword scabbard

GENERAL'S BOOTS

Buckle

Heel

Sole

OFFICER'S TROUSERS

Adjustment strap

Buckle

Fly button

Lining

Piping

INFANTRYMAN, NEW YORK VOLUNTEERS

Infantry cap cord
Infantry badge
Hardee felt hat
Bayonet
Caped overcoat
Box for percussion caps
Belt
State of New York belt buckle
Musket
Bayonet scabbard
Trousers
Woollen sock
Jefferson bootee

SERGEANT, 157TH NEW YORK VOLUNTEERS

Chin strap
Forage cap
NCO sword belt
Frock coat
Sergeant's chevrons
NCO waist belt
Eagle belt buckle
NCO sword
NCO worsted sash
Trousers
NCO trouser stripe
Shoe

CAVALRYMAN

Chin strap
Forage cap
Cavalry piping
Carbine sling
Jacket
Gauntlet
Carbine
Saber
Pistol holster
Eagle belt buckle
Saber knot
Cavalry trousers

PRIVATE, 10TH NEW YORK VOLUNTEERS

Fez
Tassel
Bayonet
Zouave jacket
Braid knotting
Waistcoat
State of New York belt buckle
Sash
Musket
Zouave trousers
Canvas legging
Shoe

PRIVATE, 146TH NEW YORK VOLUNTEERS

Fez
Tassel
Braid knotting
Zouave jacket
Bayonet
Sash
State of New York belt buckle
Scabbard
Zouave trousers
Musket
Leather legging top
Canvas legging
Shoe

33

Confederate forces

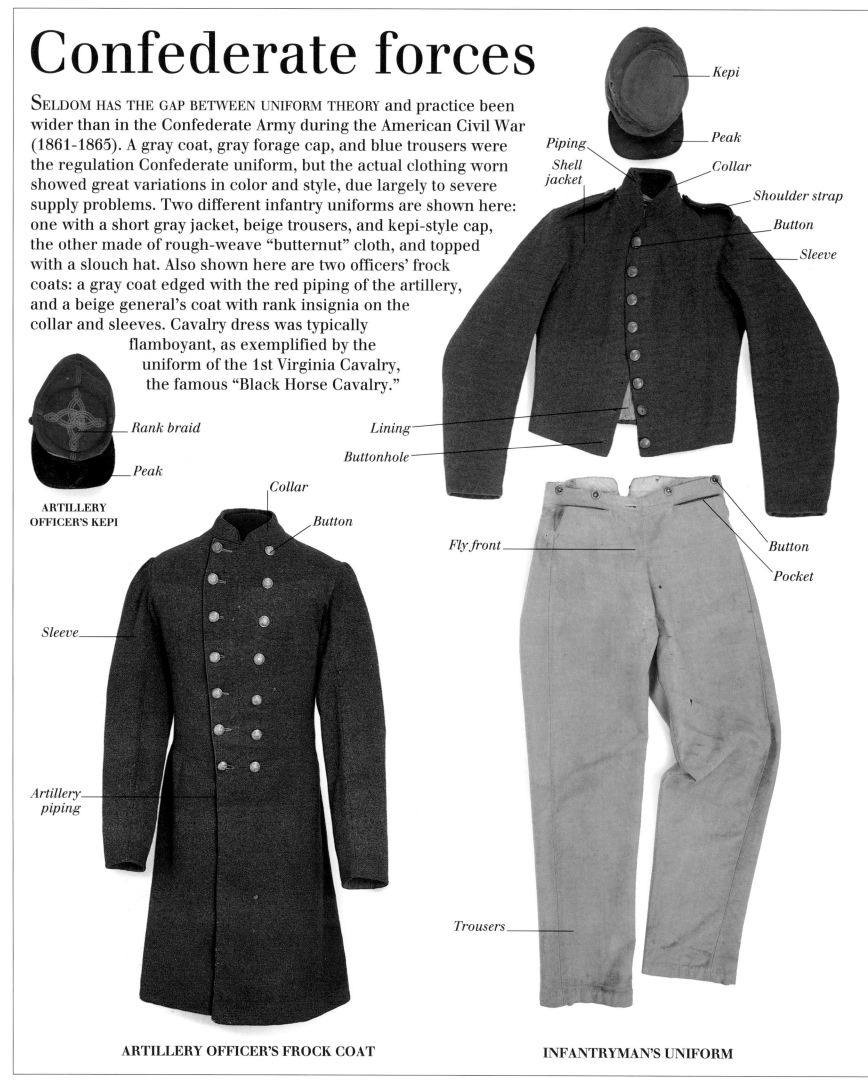

SELDOM HAS THE GAP BETWEEN UNIFORM THEORY and practice been wider than in the Confederate Army during the American Civil War (1861-1865). A gray coat, gray forage cap, and blue trousers were the regulation Confederate uniform, but the actual clothing worn showed great variations in color and style, due largely to severe supply problems. Two different infantry uniforms are shown here: one with a short gray jacket, beige trousers, and kepi-style cap, the other made of rough-weave "butternut" cloth, and topped with a slouch hat. Also shown here are two officers' frock coats: a gray coat edged with the red piping of the artillery, and a beige general's coat with rank insignia on the collar and sleeves. Cavalry dress was typically flamboyant, as exemplified by the uniform of the 1st Virginia Cavalry, the famous "Black Horse Cavalry."

Kepi

Peak

Piping

Shell jacket

Collar

Shoulder strap

Button

Sleeve

Lining

Buttonhole

Rank braid

Peak

ARTILLERY OFFICER'S KEPI

Collar

Button

Sleeve

Artillery piping

Fly front

Button

Pocket

Trousers

ARTILLERY OFFICER'S FROCK COAT

INFANTRYMAN'S UNIFORM

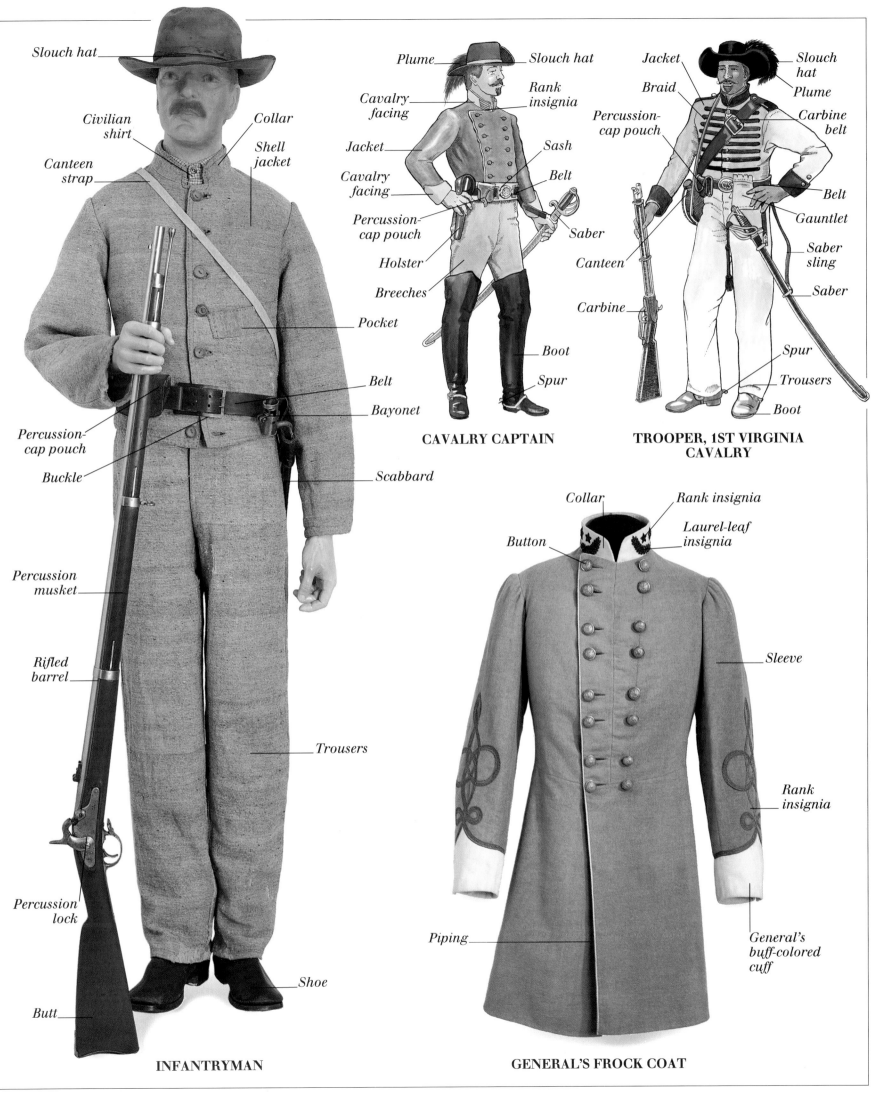

Slouch hat

Civilian shirt

Collar

Shell jacket

Canteen strap

Percussion-cap pouch

Buckle

Percussion musket

Rifled barrel

Trousers

Percussion lock

Butt

Shoe

Pocket

Belt

Bayonet

Scabbard

INFANTRYMAN

Plume

Cavalry facing

Jacket

Cavalry facing

Percussion-cap pouch

Holster

Breeches

Slouch hat

Rank insignia

Sash

Belt

Saber

Boot

Spur

CAVALRY CAPTAIN

Jacket

Braid

Percussion-cap pouch

Canteen

Carbine

Slouch hat

Plume

Carbine belt

Belt

Gauntlet

Saber sling

Saber

Spur

Trousers

Boot

TROOPER, 1ST VIRGINIA CAVALRY

Collar

Button

Piping

Rank insignia

Laurel-leaf insignia

Sleeve

Rank insignia

General's buff-colored cuff

GENERAL'S FROCK COAT

Footgear

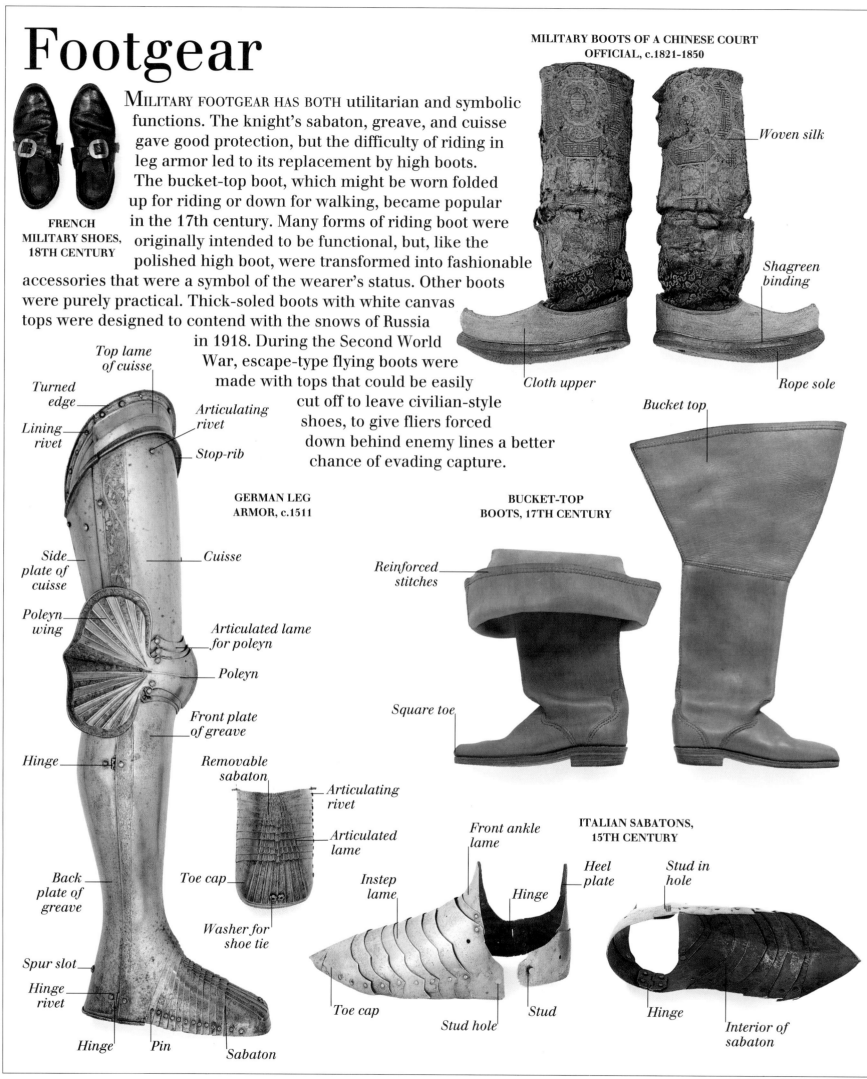

MILITARY FOOTGEAR HAS BOTH utilitarian and symbolic functions. The knight's sabaton, greave, and cuisse gave good protection, but the difficulty of riding in leg armor led to its replacement by high boots. The bucket-top boot, which might be worn folded up for riding or down for walking, became popular in the 17th century. Many forms of riding boot were originally intended to be functional, but, like the polished high boot, were transformed into fashionable accessories that were a symbol of the wearer's status. Other boots were purely practical. Thick-soled boots with white canvas tops were designed to contend with the snows of Russia in 1918. During the Second World War, escape-type flying boots were made with tops that could be easily cut off to leave civilian-style shoes, to give fliers forced down behind enemy lines a better chance of evading capture.

FRENCH MILITARY SHOES, 18TH CENTURY

MILITARY BOOTS OF A CHINESE COURT OFFICIAL, c.1821-1850

Woven silk

Shagreen binding

Cloth upper

Rope sole

GERMAN LEG ARMOR, c.1511

Top lame of cuisse

Turned edge

Lining rivet

Articulating rivet

Stop-rib

Side plate of cuisse

Cuisse

Poleyn wing

Articulated lame for poleyn

Poleyn

Front plate of greave

Hinge

Removable sabaton

Articulating rivet

Articulated lame

Back plate of greave

Toe cap

Washer for shoe tie

Spur slot

Hinge rivet

Hinge

Pin

Sabaton

BUCKET-TOP BOOTS, 17TH CENTURY

Bucket top

Reinforced stitches

Square toe

ITALIAN SABATONS, 15TH CENTURY

Front ankle lame

Heel plate

Stud in hole

Instep lame

Hinge

Toe cap

Stud hole

Stud

Hinge

Interior of sabaton

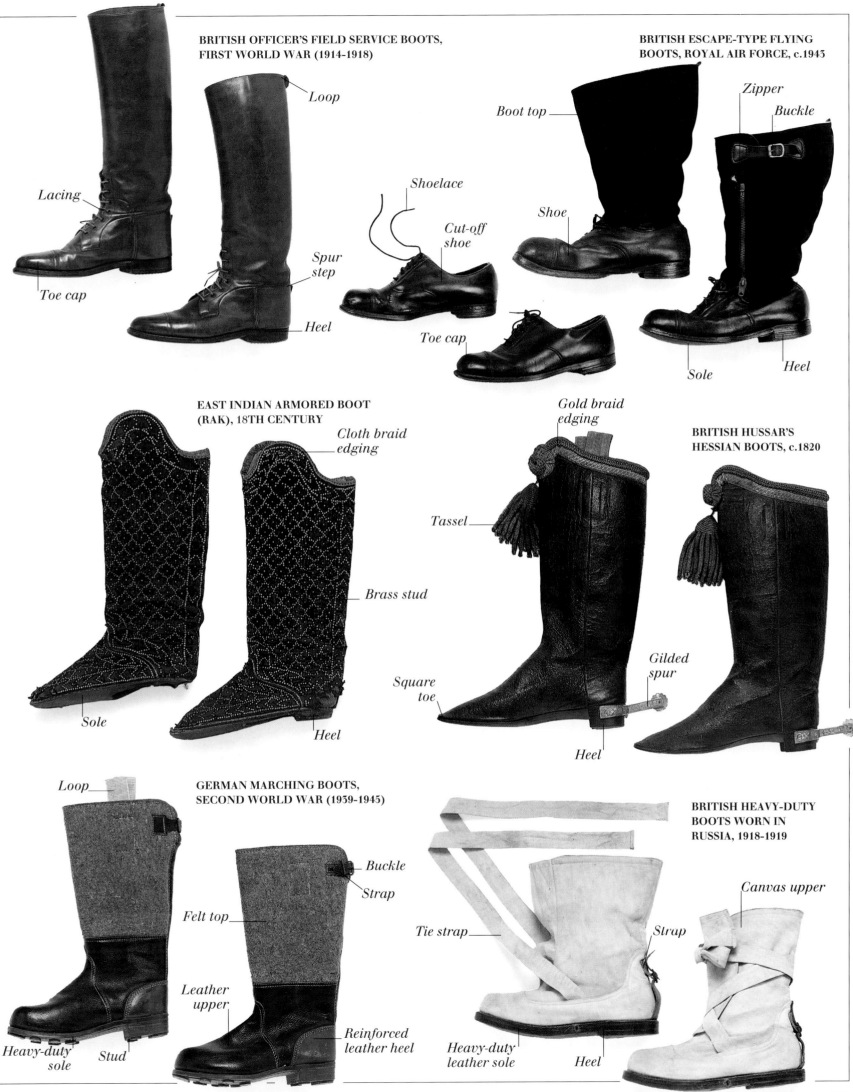

BRITISH OFFICER'S FIELD SERVICE BOOTS, FIRST WORLD WAR (1914-1918)

Loop

Lacing

Spur step

Toe cap

Heel

Shoelace

Cut-off shoe

Toe cap

BRITISH ESCAPE-TYPE FLYING BOOTS, ROYAL AIR FORCE, c.1943

Boot top

Zipper

Buckle

Shoe

Sole

Heel

EAST INDIAN ARMORED BOOT (RAK), 18TH CENTURY

Cloth braid edging

Brass stud

Sole

Heel

Gold braid edging

BRITISH HUSSAR'S HESSIAN BOOTS, c.1820

Tassel

Gilded spur

Square toe

Heel

GERMAN MARCHING BOOTS, SECOND WORLD WAR (1939-1945)

Loop

Buckle

Strap

Felt top

Leather upper

Reinforced leather heel

Heavy-duty sole

Stud

BRITISH HEAVY-DUTY BOOTS WORN IN RUSSIA, 1918-1919

Canvas upper

Tie strap

Strap

Heavy-duty leather sole

Heel

Khaki uniforms

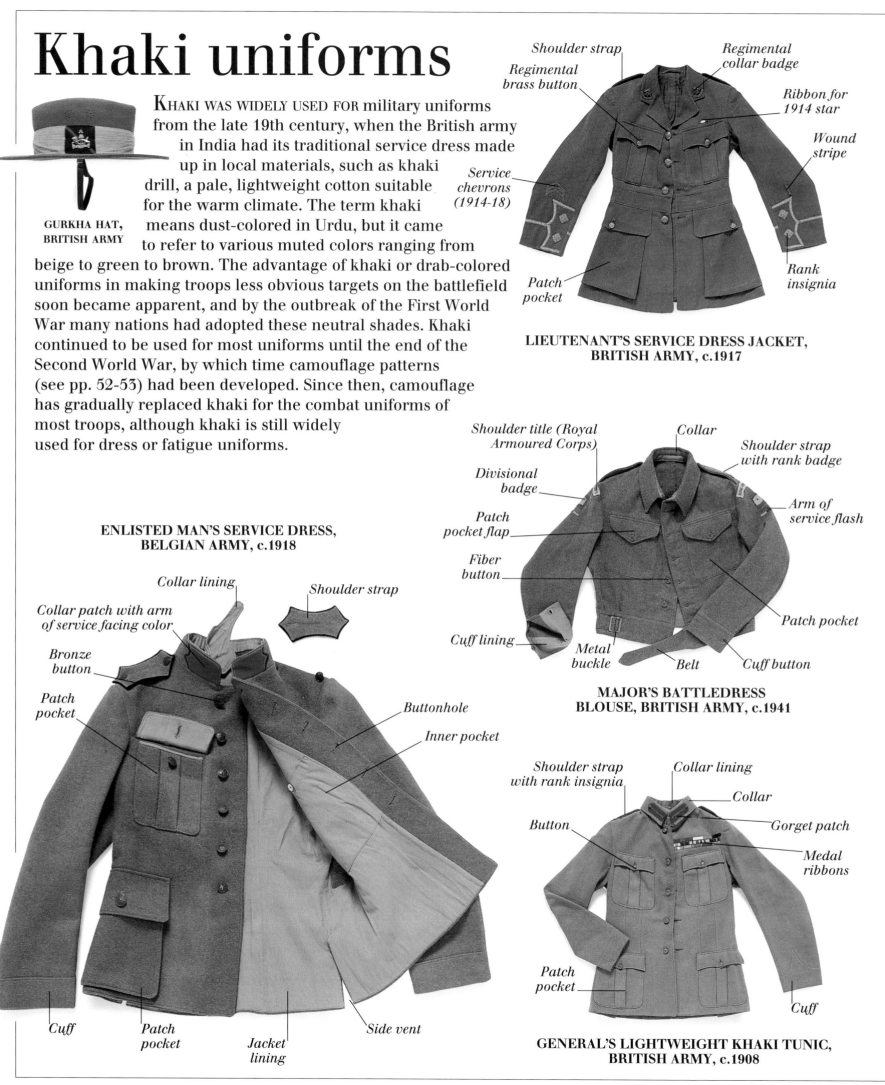

GURKHA HAT, BRITISH ARMY

Khaki was widely used for military uniforms from the late 19th century, when the British army in India had its traditional service dress made up in local materials, such as khaki drill, a pale, lightweight cotton suitable for the warm climate. The term khaki means dust-colored in Urdu, but it came to refer to various muted colors ranging from beige to green to brown. The advantage of khaki or drab-colored uniforms in making troops less obvious targets on the battlefield soon became apparent, and by the outbreak of the First World War many nations had adopted these neutral shades. Khaki continued to be used for most uniforms until the end of the Second World War, by which time camouflage patterns (see pp. 52-53) had been developed. Since then, camouflage has gradually replaced khaki for the combat uniforms of most troops, although khaki is still widely used for dress or fatigue uniforms.

Shoulder strap

Regimental brass button

Regimental collar badge

Ribbon for 1914 star

Wound stripe

Service chevrons (1914-18)

Patch pocket

Rank insignia

LIEUTENANT'S SERVICE DRESS JACKET, BRITISH ARMY, c.1917

Shoulder title (Royal Armoured Corps)

Collar

Divisional badge

Shoulder strap with rank badge

Patch pocket flap

Arm of service flash

Fiber button

Patch pocket

Cuff lining

Metal buckle

Belt

Cuff button

MAJOR'S BATTLEDRESS BLOUSE, BRITISH ARMY, c.1941

ENLISTED MAN'S SERVICE DRESS, BELGIAN ARMY, c.1918

Collar lining

Shoulder strap

Collar patch with arm of service facing color

Bronze button

Patch pocket

Buttonhole

Inner pocket

Cuff

Patch pocket

Jacket lining

Side vent

Shoulder strap with rank insignia

Collar lining

Collar

Button

Gorget patch

Medal ribbons

Patch pocket

Cuff

GENERAL'S LIGHTWEIGHT KHAKI TUNIC, BRITISH ARMY, c.1908

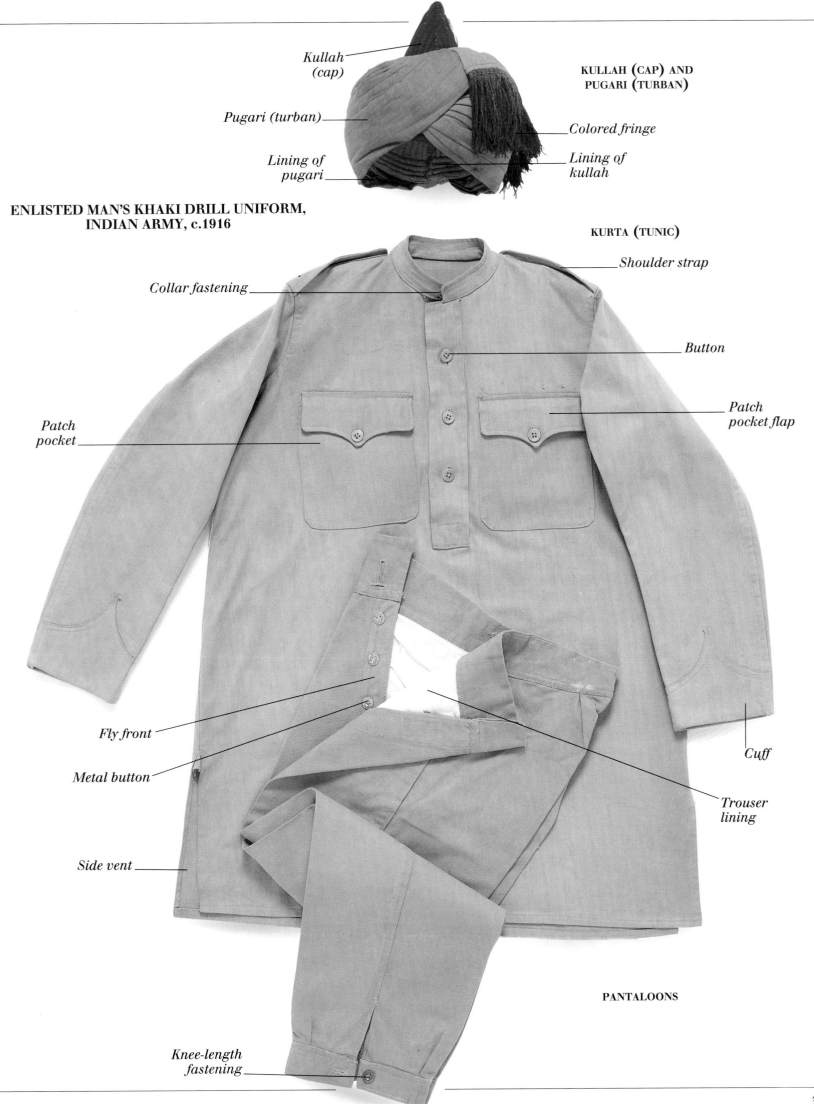

Kullah
(cap)

KULLAH (CAP) AND
PUGARI (TURBAN)

Pugari (turban)

Colored fringe

Lining of
pugari

Lining of
kullah

**ENLISTED MAN'S KHAKI DRILL UNIFORM,
INDIAN ARMY, c.1916**

KURTA (TUNIC)

Shoulder strap

Collar fastening

Button

Patch
pocket

Patch
pocket flap

Fly front

Cuff

Metal button

Trouser
lining

Side vent

PANTALOONS

Knee-length
fastening

Belts, holsters, and scabbards

ARMS, AMMUNITION, AND OTHER items of military equipment need to be carried securely and yet must also be easily accessible. Many different accoutrements have been used for this purpose, most of which were attached to the body by a belt or strap. Swords, daggers, small firearms, and ammunition were carried on belts. Swords and daggers were usually sheathed in scabbards, small firearms were held in holsters, and ammunition was carried in pouches. The "Sam Browne" belt, combining shoulder straps and a waist belt, enabled a sword and pistol to be worn comfortably at the same time. Early firearms, such as muskets, used gunpowder and shot. The gunpowder was often carried in flasks, which were attached to a belt or suspended from a chain; shot was carried in bullet pouches. Arrows were held in a quiver that was usually strapped across the back.

INDIAN POWDER FLASK

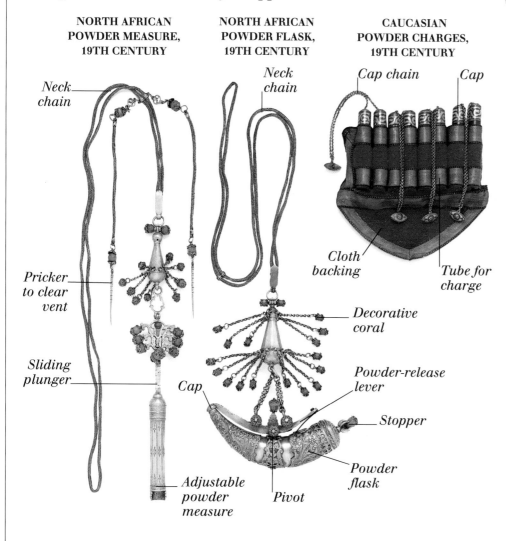

BRITISH OFFICER'S "SAM BROWNE" BELT, FIRST WORLD WAR (1914-1918)

- Leather sword knot
- Shoulder strap
- Pommel
- Grip
- Guard
- "D" ring
- Buckle
- Waist belt
- Sword hook
- Blade
- Sword frog
- Scabbard

GERMAN POWDER FLASK AND BULLET BAG, c.1600

- Belt loop
- Bullet-bag cover
- Button
- Bullet bag
- Powder-release lever
- Spring
- Pivot
- Frog
- Spout
- Powder flask
- Flask base-mount

NORTH AFRICAN POWDER MEASURE, 19TH CENTURY

- Neck chain
- Pricker to clear vent
- Sliding plunger
- Adjustable powder measure

NORTH AFRICAN POWDER FLASK, 19TH CENTURY

- Neck chain
- Decorative coral
- Cap
- Powder-release lever
- Stopper
- Powder flask
- Pivot

CAUCASIAN POWDER CHARGES, 19TH CENTURY

- Cap chain
- Cap
- Cloth backing
- Tube for charge

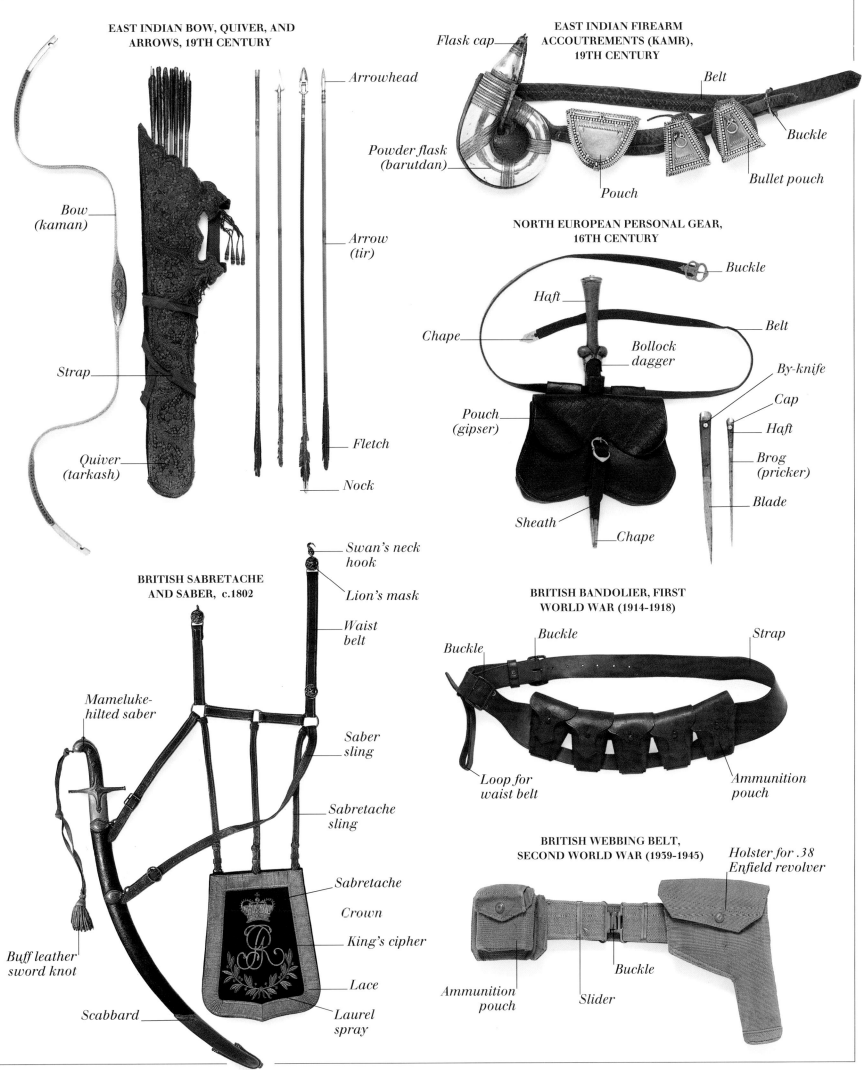

EAST INDIAN BOW, QUIVER, AND ARROWS, 19TH CENTURY

Arrowhead

Bow (kaman)

Arrow (tir)

Strap

Fletch

Quiver (tarkash)

Nock

EAST INDIAN FIREARM ACCOUTREMENTS (KAMR), 19TH CENTURY

Flask cap

Belt

Buckle

Powder flask (barutdan)

Bullet pouch

Pouch

NORTH EUROPEAN PERSONAL GEAR, 16TH CENTURY

Buckle

Haft

Belt

Chape

Bollock dagger

By-knife

Cap

Haft

Pouch (gipser)

Brog (pricker)

Blade

Sheath

Chape

BRITISH SABRETACHE AND SABER, c.1802

Swan's neck hook

Lion's mask

Waist belt

Mameluke-hilted saber

Saber sling

Sabretache sling

Sabretache

Crown

King's cipher

Buff leather sword knot

Lace

Scabbard

Laurel spray

BRITISH BANDOLIER, FIRST WORLD WAR (1914-1918)

Buckle

Buckle

Strap

Loop for waist belt

Ammunition pouch

BRITISH WEBBING BELT, SECOND WORLD WAR (1939-1945)

Holster for .38 Enfield revolver

Ammunition pouch

Buckle

Slider

First World War infantry

By the outbreak of the first world war in 1914, many armies already wore dull-colored service dress, which became increasingly utilitarian as the war progressed. Some Scottish units retained the kilt, which was worn with a doublet that had a cutaway front to accommodate the sporran (pouch). The kilt of the London Scottish battalion was a traditional, inconspicuous hodden gray color with tartan lining. In 1916 the glengarry cap was replaced by a steel helmet. The French infantry changed its dark blue coat and red trousers to the less obvious shade of horizon blue in 1915. The Germans wore field gray from the start of the war, but replaced the traditional brass and leather spiked helmet with their distinctive steel helmet in 1916.

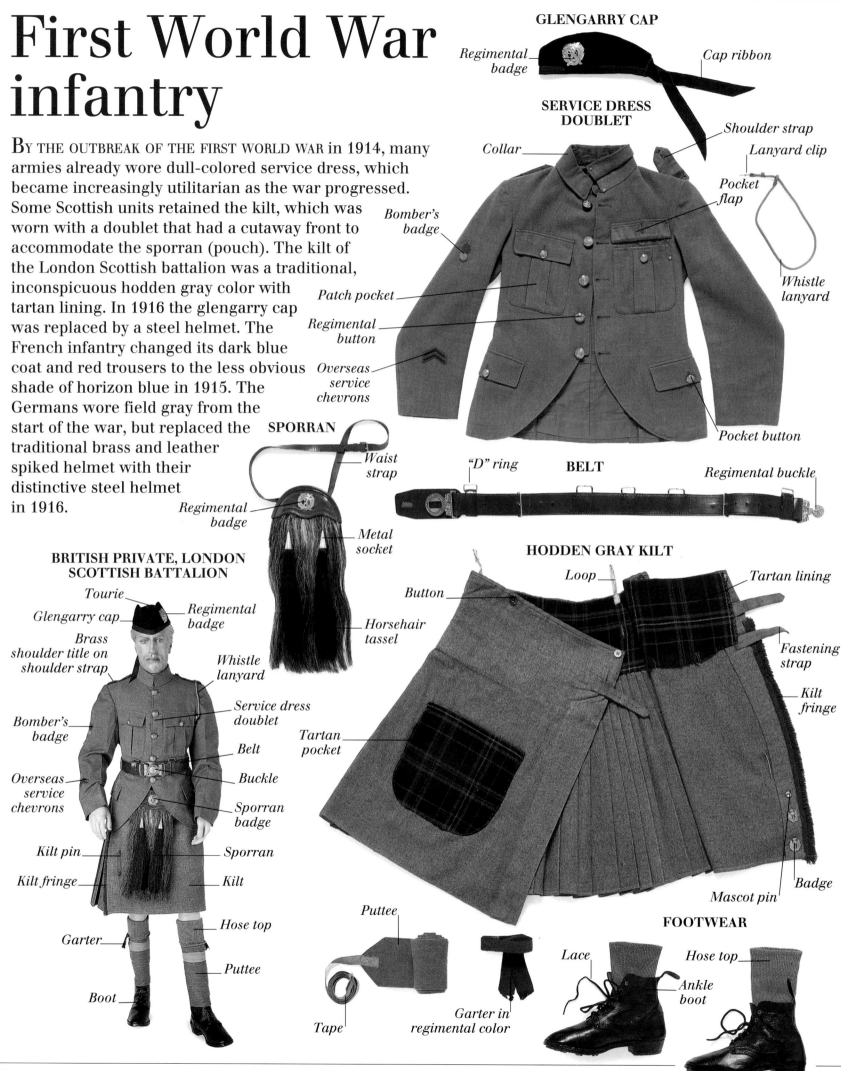

GLENGARRY CAP

Regimental badge

Cap ribbon

SERVICE DRESS DOUBLET

Collar

Shoulder strap

Lanyard clip

Pocket flap

Bomber's badge

Whistle lanyard

Patch pocket

Regimental button

Overseas service chevrons

Pocket button

SPORRAN

Waist strap

Regimental badge

Metal socket

Horsehair tassel

"D" ring

BELT

Regimental buckle

HODDEN GRAY KILT

Loop

Button

Tartan lining

Fastening strap

Kilt fringe

Tartan pocket

Mascot pin

Badge

BRITISH PRIVATE, LONDON SCOTTISH BATTALION

Tourie

Glengarry cap

Regimental badge

Brass shoulder title on shoulder strap

Whistle lanyard

Service dress doublet

Bomber's badge

Belt

Overseas service chevrons

Buckle

Sporran badge

Kilt pin

Sporran

Kilt fringe

Kilt

Garter

Hose top

Puttee

Boot

Puttee

Tape

Garter in regimental color

FOOTWEAR

Lace

Hose top

Ankle boot

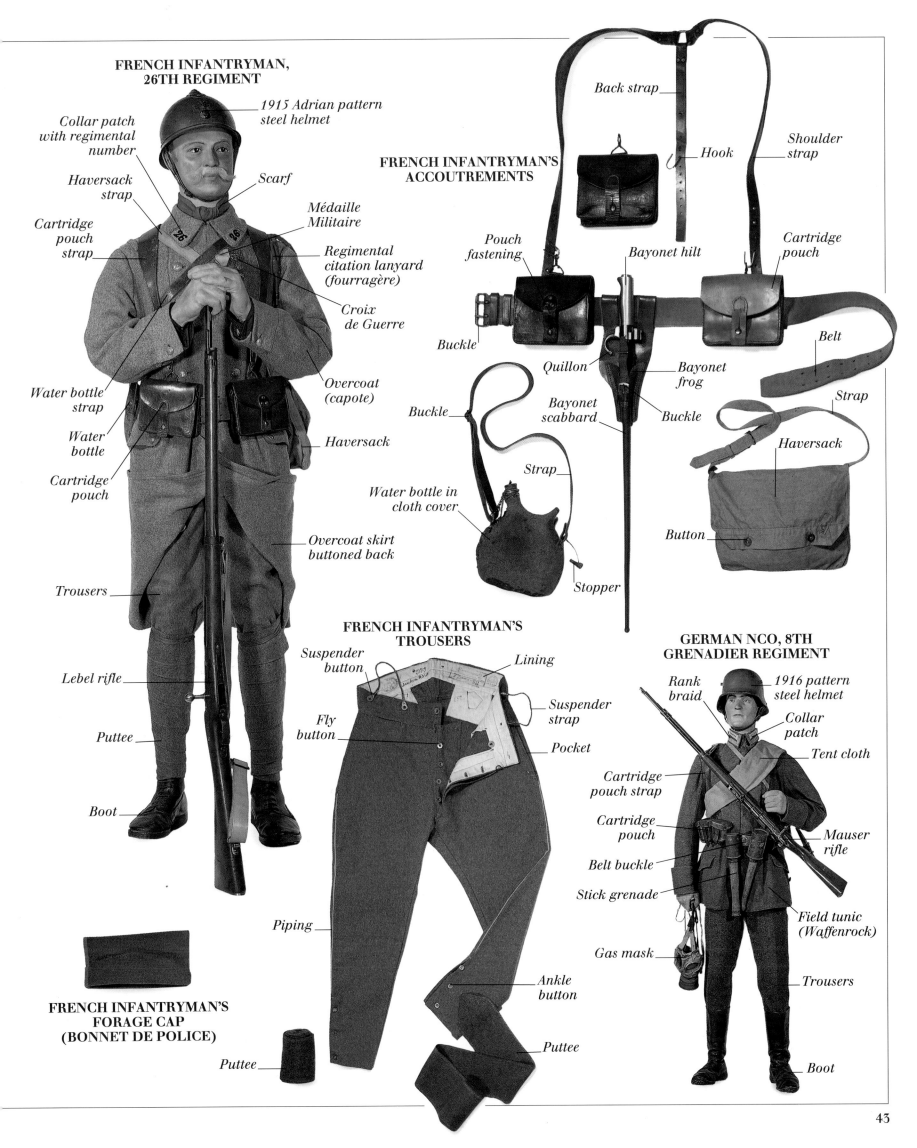

FRENCH INFANTRYMAN, 26TH REGIMENT

Collar patch with regimental number

1915 Adrian pattern steel helmet

Haversack strap

Scarf

Médaille Militaire

Cartridge pouch strap

Regimental citation lanyard (fourragère)

Croix de Guerre

Overcoat (capote)

Water bottle strap

Water bottle

Haversack

Cartridge pouch

Overcoat skirt buttoned back

Trousers

Lebel rifle

Puttee

Boot

FRENCH INFANTRYMAN'S FORAGE CAP (BONNET DE POLICE)

FRENCH INFANTRYMAN'S ACCOUTREMENTS

Back strap

Hook

Shoulder strap

Pouch fastening

Bayonet hilt

Cartridge pouch

Buckle

Quillon

Bayonet frog

Belt

Bayonet scabbard

Buckle

Strap

Buckle

Strap

Haversack

Water bottle in cloth cover

Button

Stopper

FRENCH INFANTRYMAN'S TROUSERS

Suspender button

Lining

Suspender strap

Fly button

Pocket

Piping

Ankle button

Puttee

Puttee

GERMAN NCO, 8TH GRENADIER REGIMENT

Rank braid

1916 pattern steel helmet

Collar patch

Tent cloth

Cartridge pouch strap

Cartridge pouch

Mauser rifle

Belt buckle

Stick grenade

Field tunic (Waffenrock)

Gas mask

Trousers

Boot

43

Packs and gear

GENERATIONS OF SOLDIERS have been burdened with the weight of spare clothing, water, food, cooking equipment, entrenching (digging) tools, shelters, and ammunition. Such items have commonly been carried in packs strapped to the soldier's back and also in belt pouches worn around the body. Shown here are packs and gear from three different campaigns. Members of the French Army in the 19th century carried a pack to which were strapped half a two-man tent, with pole and pegs, and a cooking or washing pot. The American Civil War soldier's knapsack, blanket roll, and canteen comprised more basic gear than the packs and personal equipment carried by infantrymen during the First World War. The U.S. infantry equipment of this period included a haversack and a pack carrier. Contained in the haversack were personal items, including a knife, fork, spoon, and cooking utensils. Attached to the pack carrier were the bayonet and entrenching tool. Fastened in the pack carrier were the blanket roll and spare items of clothing. A cartridge belt was worn around the waist to carry ammunition, a trench knife, a canteen, and field bandages.

POCKET-SIZE NOVEL FOR U.S. TROOPS, SECOND WORLD WAR (1939-1945)

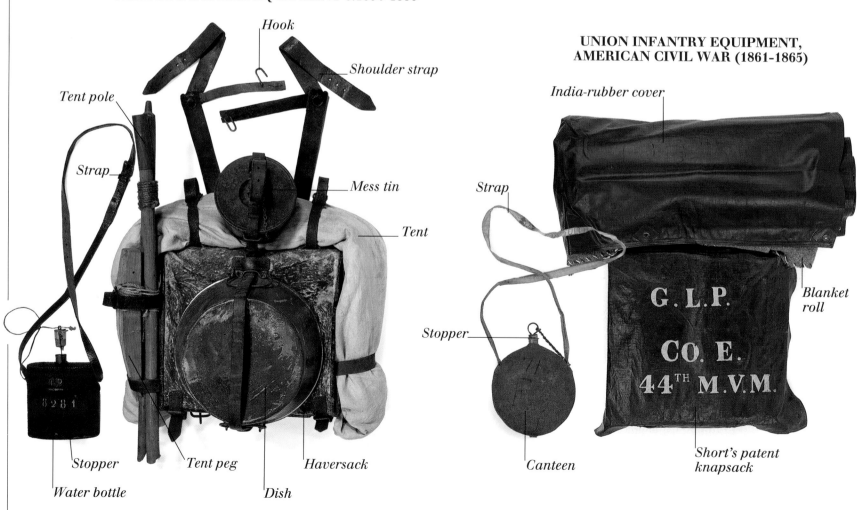

ASSEMBLED KIT, U.S. INFANTRY EQUIPMENT

M1917 Enfield bayonet handle

M1910 haversack

Suspender strap

Securing hook

M1910 entrenching tool

M1910 pack carrier

Securing strap for pack contents

Blanket or overcoat roll

FRENCH INFANTRY EQUIPMENT c.1854-1880

Hook

Shoulder strap

Tent pole

Strap

Mess tin

Tent

Stopper

Tent peg

Haversack

Water bottle

Dish

UNION INFANTRY EQUIPMENT, AMERICAN CIVIL WAR (1861-1865)

India-rubber cover

Strap

Blanket roll

Stopper

G.L.P. CO. E. 44TH M.V.M.

Canteen

Short's patent knapsack

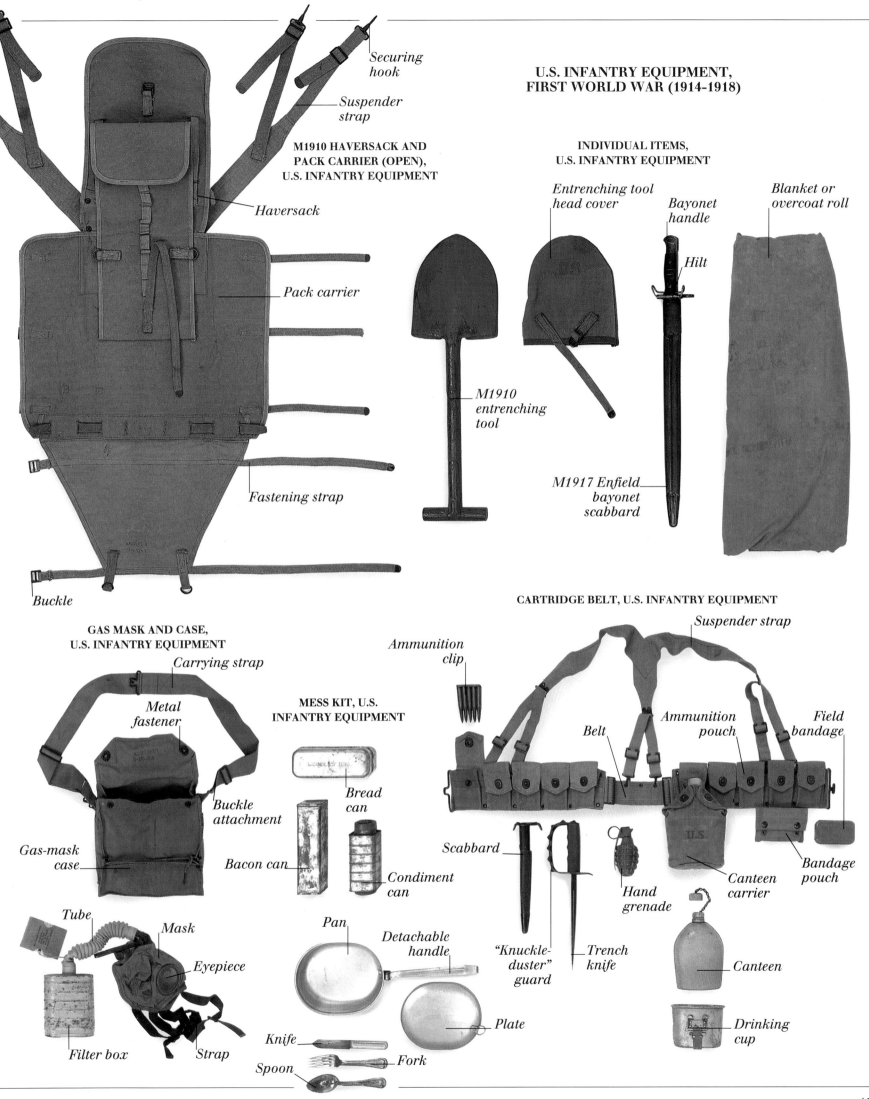

U.S. INFANTRY EQUIPMENT, FIRST WORLD WAR (1914-1918)

M1910 HAVERSACK AND PACK CARRIER (OPEN), U.S. INFANTRY EQUIPMENT

Securing hook

Suspender strap

Haversack

Pack carrier

Fastening strap

Buckle

INDIVIDUAL ITEMS, U.S. INFANTRY EQUIPMENT

Entrenching tool head cover

Bayonet handle

Blanket or overcoat roll

Hilt

M1910 entrenching tool

M1917 Enfield bayonet scabbard

GAS MASK AND CASE, U.S. INFANTRY EQUIPMENT

Carrying strap

Metal fastener

Buckle attachment

Gas-mask case

Tube

Mask

Eyepiece

Filter box

Strap

MESS KIT, U.S. INFANTRY EQUIPMENT

Bread can

Bacon can

Condiment can

Pan

Detachable handle

Knife

Spoon

Fork

Plate

CARTRIDGE BELT, U.S. INFANTRY EQUIPMENT

Ammunition clip

Suspender strap

Belt

Ammunition pouch

Field bandage

Scabbard

Hand grenade

Canteen carrier

Bandage pouch

"Knuckle-duster" guard

Trench knife

Canteen

Drinking cup

The Royal Flying Corps

THE POTENTIAL OF AIRCRAFT for reconnaissance was recognized by the British army in 1911 with the formation of the Air Battalion of the Royal Engineers, which became the Royal Flying Corps in 1912. Early aircraft had open cockpits, and so the main purpose of an aviator's clothing was to keep him warm. Fleece-lined leather flying coats were worn with long boots and with gauntlets that could be worn as mittens. Aviators also wore goggles, helmets, and masks to protect their faces. An official uniform was worn under these warm outer garments. Unlike other British officers' uniforms of this period, the aviator's service dress tunic was double-breasted and had concealed buttons and inconspicuous rank badges.

AVIATOR'S HEADGEAR

Elastic strap

Face-aperture tightening strap

Tightening strap

Fur lining

Ear roll

Nose cover

Leather mask

FACE MASK

Buckle

FLYING HELMET

Buckle

Strap

Hinge

Fur trim

Tinted lens

FLYING GOGGLES

AVIATOR'S COAT

Collar

Collar-tab button

Collar tab

Horn button

Map pocket

AVIATOR, ROYAL FLYING CORPS

Flying helmet

Ear roll

Flying goggles

Face mask

Shoulder strap

Collar

Map case

Map pocket

Belt

Cuff strap

Pocket

Flying gauntlet

Elasticated cuff

Mitten flap

Pocket

Skirt-fastening button

Flying coat

Flying boot

Instep strap

Concealed buttonhole

Button tab

Fleece lining

AVIATOR'S FLYING GAUNTLETS

Mitten flap

Elasticated wrist

Fleece lining

Mitten flap

OFFICER'S JACKET

False shirt collar

Collar stud

Shoulder strap

Captain's rank insignia

Observer's brevet

Buttonhole

Medal ribbon of 1914-15 Star

Pocket

Cuff strap

Button

OFFICER'S BREECHES

Lining

Suspender button

Fly button

Pocket

Fly

AVIATOR'S FLYING BOOTS

Fleece lining

Suspension strap

Knee strap

Buckle

Instep strap

Tightening lace at knee

Buttonhole

Button

Buttoned cuff

Buckle

Heel

Masks and faceguards

THE FACE IS ONE OF THE SOLDIER'S MOST vulnerable areas, but it is also one of the most difficult parts of the body to protect effectively. A major problem of faceguard design is the need for the wearer to breathe properly, see clearly, and speak audibly. The medieval knight's helmet had a visor that gave full protection to the face when worn down but that could be lifted for greater comfort when not in battle. Grotesque faceguards, fashionable in the 16th century, were intended to impress or terrify the beholder. Mail has been a common component of faceguards, especially in India and the Middle East, and was even worn by First World War tank crewmen. The advent of chemical warfare in the present century has made special gas masks and respirators an essential part of modern military equipment.

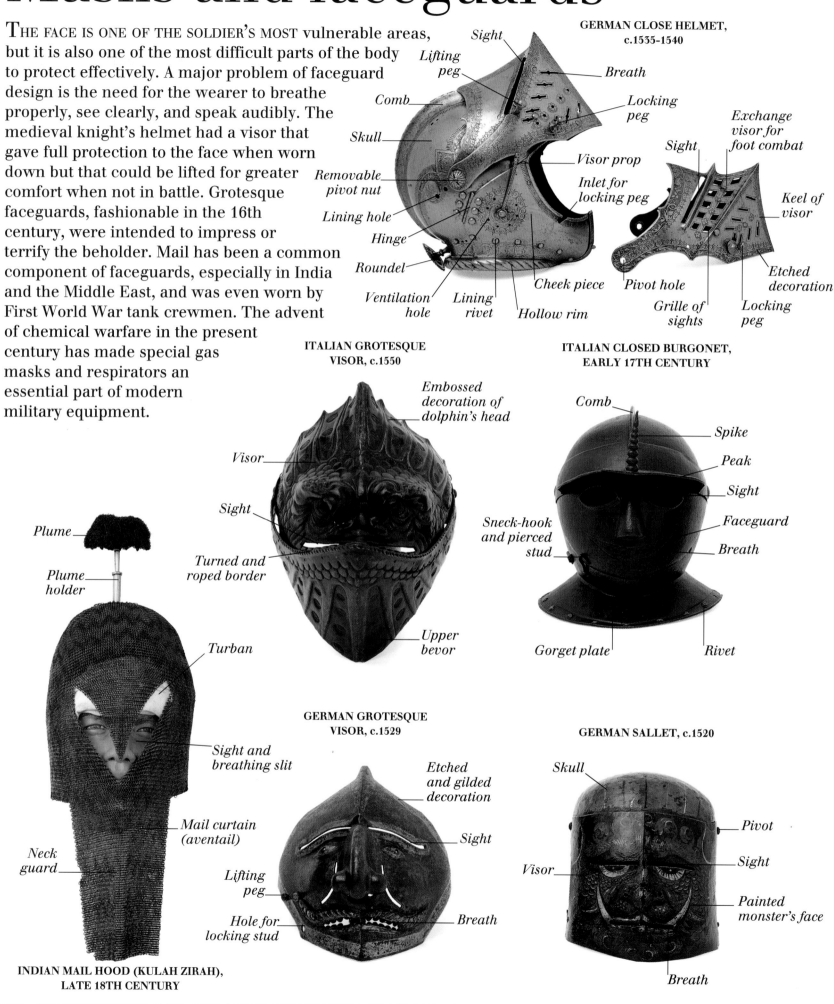

GERMAN CLOSE HELMET, c.1535-1540

Sight · Lifting peg · Comb · Skull · Removable pivot nut · Lining hole · Hinge · Roundel · Ventilation hole · Lining rivet · Breath · Locking peg · Visor prop · Inlet for locking peg · Cheek piece · Hollow rim · Exchange visor for foot combat · Sight · Keel of visor · Etched decoration · Pivot hole · Grille of sights · Locking peg

ITALIAN GROTESQUE VISOR, c.1550

Embossed decoration of dolphin's head · Visor · Sight · Turned and roped border · Upper bevor

ITALIAN CLOSED BURGONET, EARLY 17TH CENTURY

Comb · Spike · Peak · Sight · Sneck-hook and pierced stud · Faceguard · Breath · Gorget plate · Rivet

INDIAN MAIL HOOD (KULAH ZIRAH), LATE 18TH CENTURY

Plume · Plume holder · Turban · Sight and breathing slit · Mail curtain (aventail) · Neck guard

GERMAN GROTESQUE VISOR, c.1529

Etched and gilded decoration · Sight · Lifting peg · Hole for locking stud · Breath

GERMAN SALLET, c.1520

Skull · Visor · Pivot · Sight · Painted monster's face · Breath

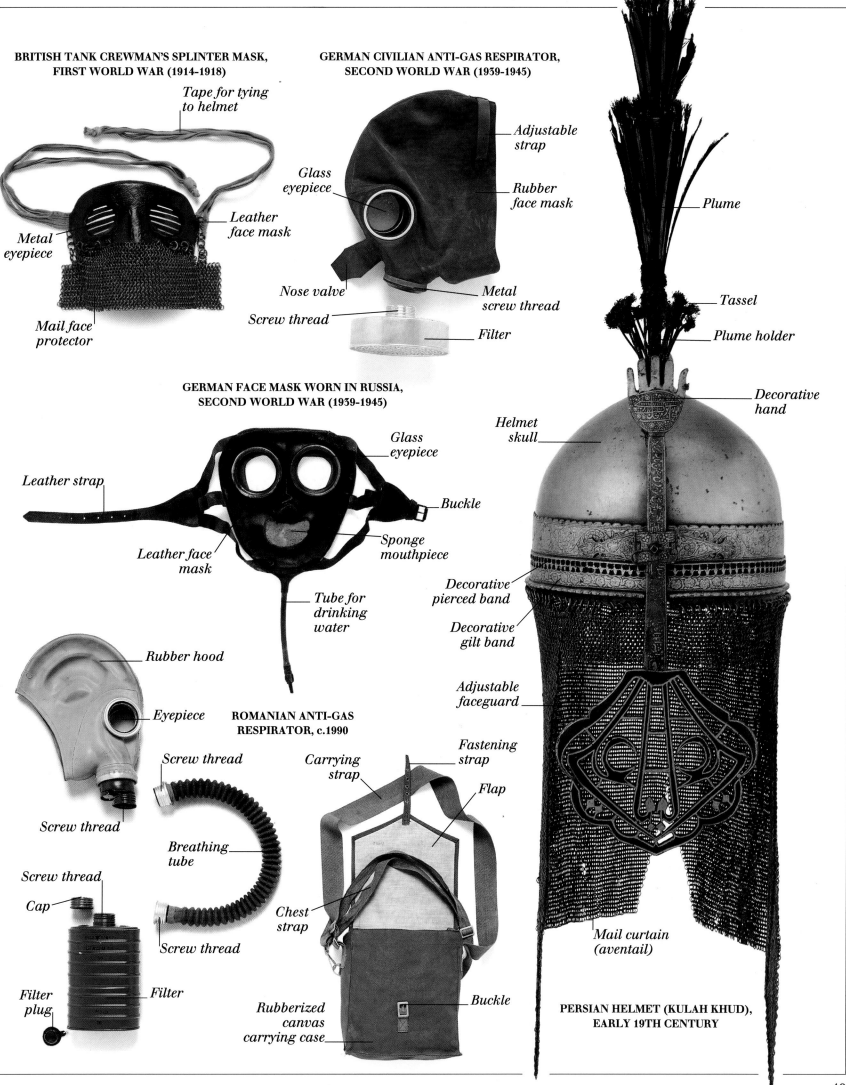

BRITISH TANK CREWMAN'S SPLINTER MASK, FIRST WORLD WAR (1914-1918)

Tape for tying to helmet

Leather face mask

Metal eyepiece

Mail face protector

GERMAN CIVILIAN ANTI-GAS RESPIRATOR, SECOND WORLD WAR (1939-1945)

Adjustable strap

Rubber face mask

Glass eyepiece

Nose valve

Metal screw thread

Screw thread

Filter

GERMAN FACE MASK WORN IN RUSSIA, SECOND WORLD WAR (1939-1945)

Glass eyepiece

Leather strap

Buckle

Leather face mask

Sponge mouthpiece

Tube for drinking water

Rubber hood

Eyepiece

Screw thread

Screw thread

Breathing tube

Screw thread

Cap

Screw thread

Filter plug

Filter

ROMANIAN ANTI-GAS RESPIRATOR, c.1990

Carrying strap

Fastening strap

Flap

Chest strap

Rubberized canvas carrying case

Buckle

Plume

Tassel

Plume holder

Decorative hand

Helmet skull

Decorative pierced band

Decorative gilt band

Adjustable faceguard

Mail curtain (aventail)

PERSIAN HELMET (KULAH KHUD), EARLY 19TH CENTURY

Hitler's army

**PRIVATE, SS PANZER DIVISION
"LEIBSTANDARTE ADOLF HITLER"**

GERMAN SECOND WORLD WAR GROUND FORCES included both the regular army and the Waffen-SS. (The Waffen-SS were the combat divisions of the Shutzstaffel–commonly known as the SS–the security force created by Adolf Hitler to consolidate the power of the National Socialist Party.) German uniforms of this period combined innovation with tradition. On their caps and jackets, army officers and men wore the new national emblem (Hoheitsabzeichen) of an eagle clutching an oak-leaf wreath encircling a swastika. They also kept some traditional features and insignia, such as the general's gold-on-scarlet collar patches. Piping (Waffenfarbe) of different colors identified each branch of the army. For example, the General Staff wore carmine, the infantry wore white, and the artillery wore red. Panzer (tank) troops had a completely different uniform from other branches of the army, with a short, close-fitting jacket (Panzerjacke) that was suited to the cramped conditions inside a tank. Members of the SS could be identified by their unique victory runes (Siegrunen), and had their own rank and unit markings. Cuff titles showing the wearer's division were also widely used by the SS but were less common in the rest of the army.

**SS ARMBAND
(SS KAMFBINDE)**

Field cap

Scarf

Victory runes

Panzer jacket

Belt

Glove

Rank collar patch

National emblem

Cuff title

Trousers

Boot

**FIELD CAP
(FELDMÜTZE), 1940**

*National emblem
(Hoheitsabzeichen)*

*Death's head emblem
(Totenkopfabzeichen)*

**PANZER JACKET
(PANZERJACKE)**

*Collar patch with victory
runes (Siegrunen)*

*Shoulder
strap*

*Piping (Waffenfarbe)
of the panzer division*

*Divisional
badge*

*Collar patch for
private (SS Schütze)*

*National
emblem*

Eagle

*Oak-leaf
wreath*

Swastika

Pocket

*Internal
fastening*

*Cuff title
"Adolf Hitler"*

Sleeve

Button

Belt support strap

Drawstring

BELT AND TROUSERS

*Buckle motto
"Meine Ehre heisst Treue"
("Loyalty is my honor")*

Loop

Pocket flap

*Belt
webbing*

Fly front

Edging

*Ankle
slit*

BOOTS

*Leather
bootlace*

Sole

Heel

General officer's cap

MAJOR GENERAL, PANZER GRENADIER REGIMENT "GROSSDEUTSCHLAND"

Rank badge

National emblem

General officer's collar patch

Ribbon bar

Iron Cross

Belt

Cuff title

Infantry assault badge

Field service tunic

Holster

Breeches

Boot

Leather strap

Gilt buckle

Holster

GENERAL OFFICER'S BREECHES AND BELT

Watch pocket

Suspender button

Adjustable waist strap

Pocket slit

Pocket button

Fly front

Fly button

Broad red stripe for general officer

Calf lacing

National emblem (Hoheitsabzeichen)

Eagle

Swastika

GENERAL OFFICER'S CAP (SCHIRMMÜTZE)

Oak-leaf wreath

Button

Oak and laurel leaves

Cap cord

Plastic peak

Cockade

FIELD SERVICE TUNIC (FELDBLUSE)

Collar

Rank badge for Major General

Gold oak-leaf collar patch for general officer

Ribbon bar

Pocket flap

National emblem

Patch pocket

Button

Iron Cross 1st Class, 1939

GENERAL OFFICER'S BOOTS

Buckle

Hook for dress dagger

Lining

Sole

Heel

Cuff title "Grossdeutschland"

Internal buckle

Internal belt

Camouflage

ONE OF THE MAIN PURPOSES OF MODERN COMBAT uniforms is concealment. Camouflage achieves this by breaking up the outline of the soldier and helping him to blend in with the background. Camouflage was used to a limited extent in the Second World War, often by elite troops such as the Waffen-SS of the German army, the British airborne forces, and the U.S. Marine Corps. Since then, camouflage has been adopted by the armed forces of most nations. The colors and disruptive patterns used in camouflage are extremely diverse, reflecting the wide range of environments in which modern forces operate. Specific patterns have been designed for each of the different types of environment. For example, jungle camouflage has patches of muted shades of green, beige, and brown to provide concealment in dense vegetation, while urban camouflage has gray and white patches to blend in with modern buildings. Desert camouflage, which was worn in the Gulf War, is predominantly beige and brown to blend in with the sandy colors of the terrain.

SOUTH VIETNAMESE ARMY, JUNGLE CAMOUFLAGE

Jungle hat

Camouflage shirt

Pocket

Divisional badge

Patch pocket

Patch pocket

Buttoned pocket flap

U.S. pattern belt

Metal fastening

Patch pocket

Trousers

Patch pocket

BRITISH BODY ARMOR, DESERT CAMOUFLAGE

CZECHOSLOVAKIAN ARMY COMBAT JACKET

Hood

Drawstring fastening

Neck flap

Button

Lining

Tab

Inner pocket flap

Patch pocket flap

Drawstring

Weatherproof cuff fastening

Inner pocket flap

Button

Army issue marking

Waist fastening

Cuff button

52

U.S. ARMY COMBAT UNIFORM, DESERT CAMOUFLAGE

M-16 rifle

"Fritz" kevlar helmet with cover

Chin strap

T-shirt

Flashlight

Rifle sling

Unit badge

Stars and Stripes

Name tape

Suspender strap

Canteen

Personal equipment belt

Hat

Desert camouflage shirt

Pocket

Pocket

Trousers

Desert boot

GERMAN DEMOCRATIC REPUBLIC (NATIONALE VOLKES ARMEE) "RAINDROP" PATTERN COMBAT JACKET

Shoulder strap with rank insignia

Collar

Nationale Volkes Armee mark

Inner pistol pocket

Sleeve pocket

Pocket

Foul-weather cuff fastening

Pocket

Inner pocket

Issue number

U.S. ARMY COMBAT JACKET, URBAN PATTERN CAMOUFLAGE

Drawstring

Hood

Shoulder strap

Hood pocket

Patch pocket

Velcro fastening

Velcro fastening

Foul-weather cuff

Pocket flap

FRENCH FOREIGN LEGION PARATROOPER COMBAT JACKET

Shoulder strap

Collar

Label

Collar flap

Pocket flap

Pocket fastener

Cuff fastening

Velcro strip

Drawstring waist fastening

Patch pocket

Buttoned pocket flap

War in Vietnam

Camouflage
helmet cover

**U.S. ARMY
BADGE,
VIETNAM**

DURING THE VIETNAM WAR (1961-1973), the United
States and the South Vietnamese armies fought
against the combined forces of the North
Vietnamese regular army and the irregular
Vietcong guerrillas. Much of the fighting took
place in jungle, so most U.S. infantrymen wore
a green cotton uniform and camouflage-pattern
helmet cover. American soldiers
were well-equipped and well-armed. They
carried an ALICE (All-Purpose Lightweight
Individual Carrying Equipment) pack, which
contained rations and other items, and they
wore cloth bandoliers to carry ammunition.
In contrast, the North Vietnamese army and the
Vietcong were lightly armed and simply dressed.
The regular North Vietnamese troops wore khaki
and the Vietcong black; both wore sandals and
carried rice in a scarf sewn to form a tube.

Steel helmet

Combat
infantry badge

"Baseball"
grenade

Quick-release
shoulder harness

Fragmentation
grenade

Light anti-tank
weapon (LAW)

Name tape

Sergeant's
chevrons

Cloth
bandolier

M-16 rifle

Entrenching
tool

Jungle fatigue
shirt

Cargo
pocket

Pocket

Jungle fatigue
trousers

Canvas-topped
jungle boot

Sole with
steel plate

U.S. ARMY
COMBAT EQUIPMENT

Quick-release
shoulder harness

ALICE
pack

Water
bottle

Smoke
grenade

Poncho

Entrenching
tool cover

Entrenching
tool

Strap

Claymore
mine pack

Back strap

20-round
magazine

Bandolier

54

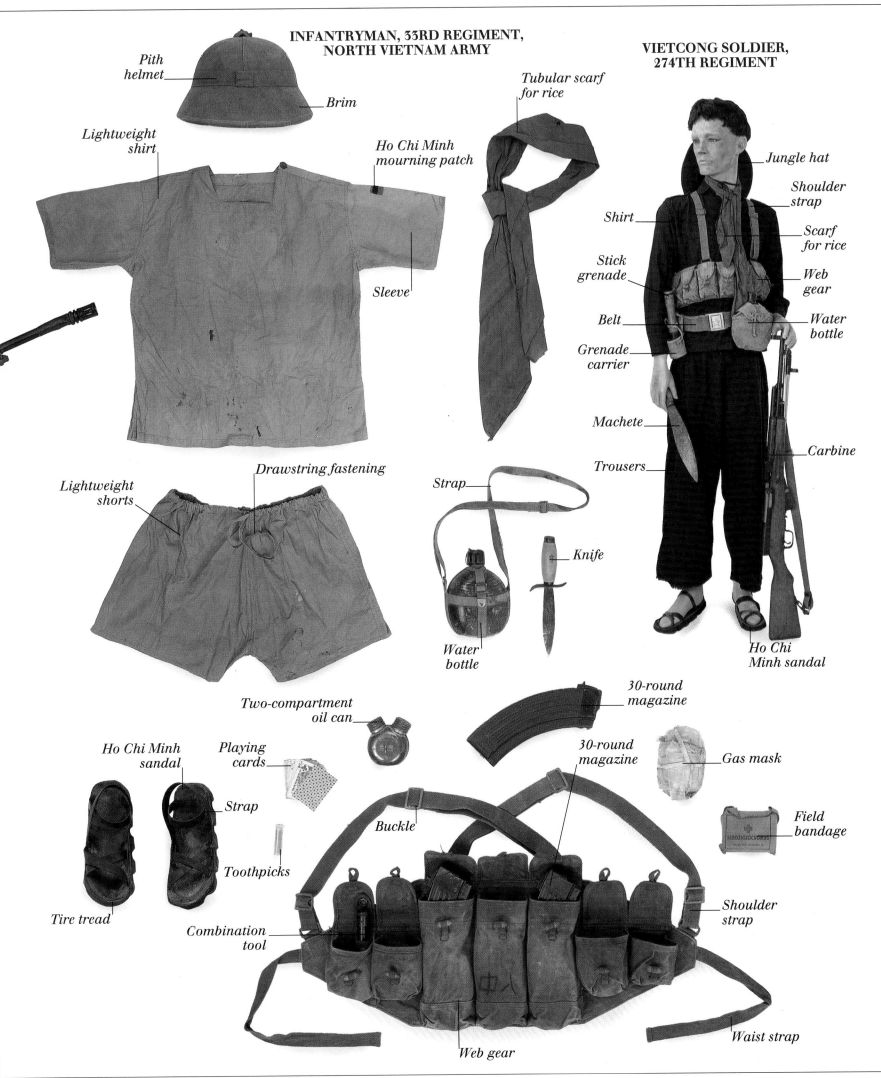

INFANTRYMAN, 33RD REGIMENT,
NORTH VIETNAM ARMY

VIETCONG SOLDIER,
274TH REGIMENT

Pith helmet

Brim

Lightweight shirt

Tubular scarf for rice

Ho Chi Minh mourning patch

Sleeve

Jungle hat

Shoulder strap

Shirt

Scarf for rice

Stick grenade

Web gear

Belt

Water bottle

Grenade carrier

Machete

Carbine

Trousers

Drawstring fastening

Lightweight shorts

Strap

Knife

Water bottle

Ho Chi Minh sandal

Two-compartment oil can

30-round magazine

Ho Chi Minh sandal

Playing cards

30-round magazine

Gas mask

Strap

Buckle

Field bandage

Toothpicks

Combination tool

Shoulder strap

Tire tread

Web gear

Waist strap

Modern naval forces

ROYAL CANADIAN NAVY BUTTON

ROYAL AUSTRALIAN NAVY BUTTON

THE UNIFORMS OF MANY MODERN NAVIES share similar features. The Soviet sailor's uniform, with its peakless cap, blue and white striped shirt, square collar, short sweater, and wide trousers provides an example of a traditional style of naval dress common to many countries. Cap ribbons generally identify the ship on which an individual sailor serves. The U.S. Navy captain, with his white and blue peaked cap, double-breasted jacket, shirt, tie, and trousers, wears a typical naval officer's uniform. National differences can be seen in badge and button designs, and also in sleeve insignia. For example, the U.S. Navy officer has a star above his gold-lace stripes, while an officer in Britain's Royal Navy has a circle added to the upper stripe. Marines are the navy's soldiers. The uniform of the Royal Netherlands Marine shown here is typical because it closely resembles an army uniform but has an anchor cap badge to show the naval connection.

SAILOR'S CAP, SOVIET NAVY

Red star cap badge

ВОЕННО-МОРСКОЙ ФЛОТ

Cap ribbon

Sleeve

Gilt button embossed with an anchor

Cuff

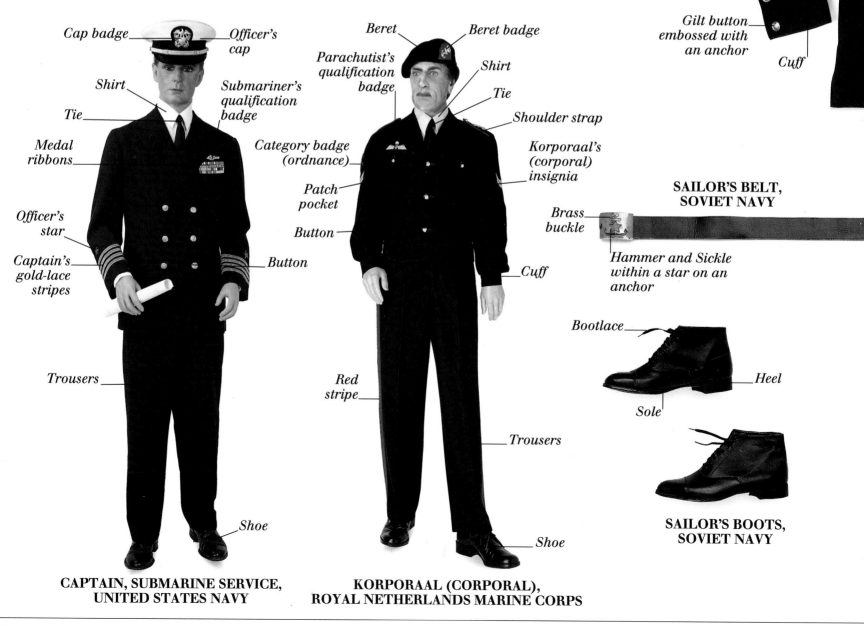

Cap badge

Officer's cap

Shirt

Submariner's qualification badge

Tie

Medal ribbons

Category badge (ordnance)

Patch pocket

Button

Officer's star

Captain's gold-lace stripes

Button

Trousers

Shoe

Beret

Beret badge

Parachutist's qualification badge

Shirt

Tie

Shoulder strap

Korporaal's (corporal) insignia

Cuff

Red stripe

Trousers

Shoe

SAILOR'S BELT, SOVIET NAVY

Brass buckle

Hammer and Sickle within a star on an anchor

Bootlace

Heel

Sole

SAILOR'S BOOTS, SOVIET NAVY

CAPTAIN, SUBMARINE SERVICE, UNITED STATES NAVY

KORPORAAL (CORPORAL), ROYAL NETHERLANDS MARINE CORPS

SAILOR'S SWEATER, SHIRT, AND COLLAR, SOVIET NAVY

Denim collar

Striped shirt

Sailor's badge

Trade badge

Sweater

Side vent

White edging

SAILOR'S DENIM COLLAR, SOVIET NAVY

Buttonhole

Seamed collar

Sleeve

SAILOR'S STRIPED SHIRT, SOVIET NAVY

SAILOR'S TROUSERS, SOVIET NAVY

Fastening clip

Fly button

Waistband

Belt loop

Pocket lining

Fall fly

Buttonhole

Collar

Sailor's badge

Trade badge

Sleeve

Gilt button

Cuff

SAILOR'S SWEATER, SOVIET NAVY

Jet aircrew

MODERN FLYING CLOTHING IS DESIGNED to keep aircrew alive in the extreme conditions of the high altitudes and speeds reached by modern jet planes. The Personal Equipment Connector links the aircrew to life-support systems in the plane. It provides oxygen to the mask and maintains the pressure in the Anti-G trousers, which counter the effects of the force (called the G-force) experienced by aircrew maneuvring at high speed. The Personal Equipment Connector also links the intercom system to the microphone in the oxygen mask and to the earphones in the flying helmet. The helmet is padded to protect the head and has clear and tinted visors. Writing pads, map pockets, and pens are positioned on the trousers and sleeves for easy access. In case the crew has to eject, they wear lifejackets containing survival aids and devices to attract rescuers.

AIRCREWMAN'S LIFEJACKET

FLIGHT LIEUTENANT, BRITISH ROYAL AIR FORCE

Flying helmet

Visor

Oxygen mask

Lifejacket

Pressure clamp

Collar

Oxygen supply hose

Handle to inflate collar

Cold-weather jacket

Glove

Personal Equipment Connector

Anti-G trousers

Writing pad

Ejector seat leg-restraint garter

Pocket

Pocket

Boot

FLIGHT SUIT

Attachment ring for Personal Equipment Connector

Shoulder strap

Pen holder

Access pocket

Adjustable waist strap

Velcro tab

Adjustable cuff strap

Pen holder

Writing pad

Pocket

Pocket

Zipper

Vent flap

ANTI-G FLYING TROUSERS

Belly band

Compressed-air input hose

Tightening lace

Safety knife scabbard

Writing pad

Pen holder

Knee hole

Pocket for survival kit

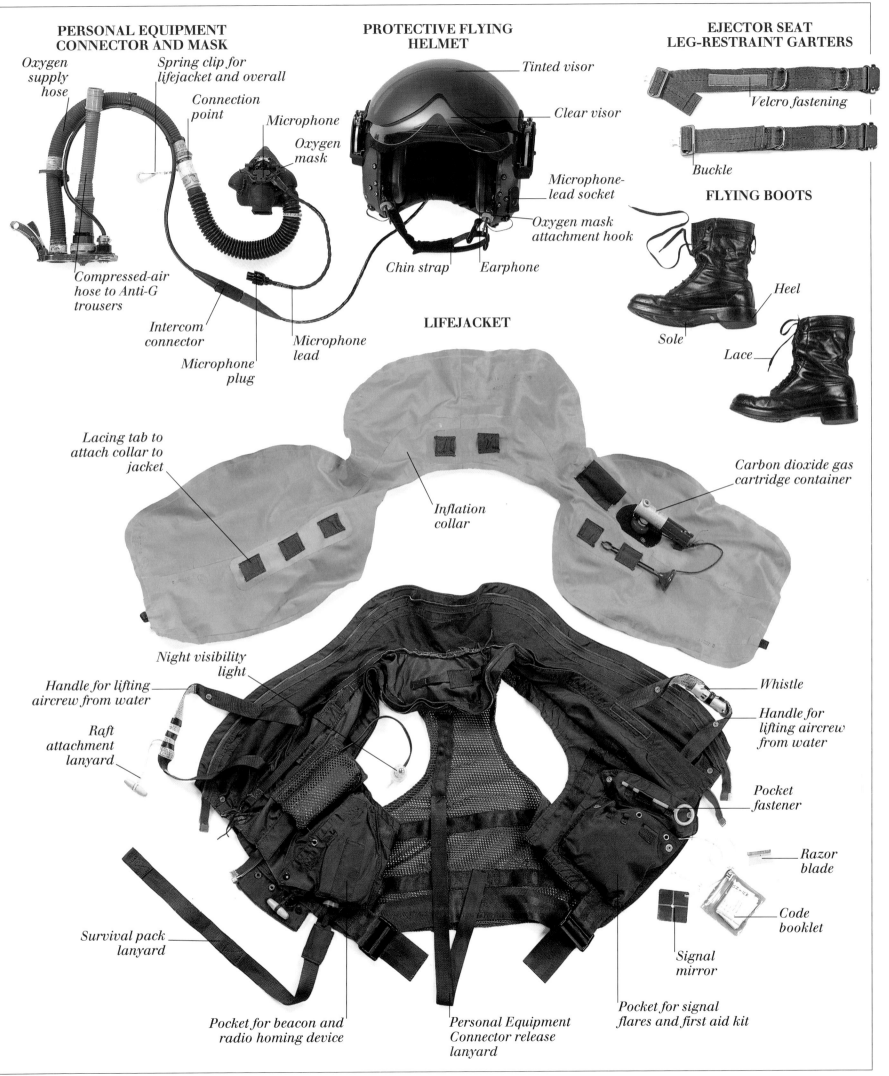

PERSONAL EQUIPMENT CONNECTOR AND MASK

Oxygen supply hose

Spring clip for lifejacket and overall

Connection point

Microphone

Oxygen mask

Compressed-air hose to Anti-G trousers

Intercom connector

Microphone plug

Microphone lead

PROTECTIVE FLYING HELMET

Tinted visor

Clear visor

Microphone-lead socket

Oxygen mask attachment hook

Chin strap

Earphone

EJECTOR SEAT LEG-RESTRAINT GARTERS

Velcro fastening

Buckle

FLYING BOOTS

Heel

Sole

Lace

LIFEJACKET

Lacing tab to attach collar to jacket

Inflation collar

Carbon dioxide gas cartridge container

Night visibility light

Handle for lifting aircrew from water

Raft attachment lanyard

Whistle

Handle for lifting aircrew from water

Pocket fastener

Razor blade

Code booklet

Signal mirror

Survival pack lanyard

Pocket for beacon and radio homing device

Personal Equipment Connector release lanyard

Pocket for signal flares and first aid kit

Index

A

- Abumi-zure (samurai leather greave covering) 13
- Accoutrements 40-41
  - French infantryman 43
- Adrian pattern helmet 43
- Aesculapius' rod 27
- Africa Star 30
- Aibiki-no-kohaze (samurai toggle) 12
- Aibiki-no-o (samurai shoulder cord) 13
- Aiguillette 15
- Air battalion 46
- Airborne forces 27
- Aircraft 46
- Aircrew **58-59**
- ALICE pack 54
- "Alliance" cockade 21
- American campaign mouche 21
- American Civil War 32, 34
  - Infantry equipment 44
  - Union hat 19
  - Union shoulder strap 27
- American infantry 21
  - Equipment 44
  - Union officer 19
- American Revolution **20-21**
- Ammunition 40
  - U.S. infantry 44-45, 54
- Ammunition pouch 41
- Anchor badge 56
  - Royal Navy 19
- Ankle boot 42
- Ankle button 43
- Ankle lame
  - English greave 9
  - Italian sabaton 36
- Anti-G trousers 58
- Anti-gas respirator 49
- Anti-tank weapon 54
- Appliqué 26
- Appliqué patch 11
- Apron
  - Greek Evzone 14
  - Roman 6
- Arm defense
  - Chinese 11
  - Samurai 12
- Arm harness 8-9
- Armband 50
- Armor **10-11**
  - Harquebusier 16
  - Leg armor 36
  - Middle Ages 8
  - Roman 6-7
  - Samurai 12-13
- Armored boot 11, 37
- Armored Brigade 27
- Armored Division 27
- Armorer 8
- Arms 40
- Army
  - Austrian 24
  - Belgian 38
  - British 27
  - Continental 21
  - Hitler's 50-51
  - Napoleon's 24
  - Roman 6-7
  - U.S. 27
- Army badges 26-27
- Army issue marking 52
- Army shoulder straps 27
- Arrows 40-41
- Artillery
  - Confederate Army 34
  - German army 50
- Astrakhan beret 19
- Austrian army 24
- Austrian Kaiserjäger officer 19
- Auxiliary cavalryman 6
- Aventail (mail curtain) 18
  - Indian 11, 48
  - Persian 10, 49
- Aviator 46

B

- Back strap 43
- Backplate
  - Harquebusier 17
  - Persian 10
  - Pikeman 16
  - Samurai 13
- Bacon can 45
- Badges 26-27
  - Union officer's hat 19
  - Bomber 42
  - British battledress 38
  - British cavalry helmet 20
  - British service dress 38
  - German Waffen-SS 27
  - Glengarry cap 42
  - Headgear 18, 27
  - London Scottish battalion 42
  - New York Volunteers 33
  - Order of the Garter 15
  - Royal Flying Corps 46
  - Royal Netherlands Marine 56
  - Russian grenadier 24
  - South Vietnamese army 52
  - Soviet sailor 56-57
  - Sporran 42
  - Trade 27
  - U.S. Army 53
  - U.S. infantryman 54
  - U.S. Navy 56
- Baldric 17
- Ball button 22-23
- Balteus (Roman sword strap) 6-7
- Bandolier
  - British 41
  - Musketeer 16
  - U.S. infantryman 54
- Bar 30-31
- Barrel sash 22
- Barutdan (Indian powder flask) 11, 41
- Base mount 40
- "Baseball" grenade 54
- Baton decoration 26
- Battle honors
  - Prussian helmet 27
  - Royal Lancers 15
- Battle of Trafalgar 28
- Battledress blouse 38
- Bavarian Order of Maximilian 15
- Bayonet
  - American infantry 21
  - Coldstream Guards 20
  - Confederate Army 35
  - French fusilier 25
  - French grenadier 21
  - French infantry 43
  - French navy 28
  - New York Volunteers 33
  - U.S. infantry 44-45
- Beacon homing device 59
- Bear's paw lace 24
- Bearskin cap
  - British grenadier 20
  - French grenadier 24
  - Hungarian grenadier 24
- Belfast 31
- Belgian army 38
- Bell-top shako 19
- Bellerophon 27
- Belly band 58
- Belt **40-41**
  - American infantry 21
  - British 38, 41
  - Carabinier 23
  - Confederate Army 35
  - French grenadier 21, 24
  - French infantryman 43
  - French navy 28
  - German NCO 43
  - German Panzer troops 50-51
  - Hussar 22-23
  - Indian 41
  - London Scottish battalion 42
  - Musketeer 16
  - New York Volunteers 33
  - North European 41
  - Royal Flying Corps 46
  - Royalist 17
  - South Vietnamese army 52
  - Soviet sailor 56-57
  - Swiss Guard 14
  - Union forces 32
  - U.S. Army combat uniform 53
  - U.S. infantry equipment 45
  - Vietcong 54
- Belt loop 40
- Belt pouch 44
- Beret 18
  - Greek Evzone 14
  - Royal Netherlands Marine 56
  - Royal Tank Regiment 19
- Bevor 48
- Bicorn hat
  - Union officer 19
  - French grenadier 21
- Binding 36
- "Black Horse Cavalry" 34
- Blade
  - British sword 40
  - North European by-knife 41
  - Roman dagger 6
  - Samurai sword 13
- Blanket roll 44-45
- Body armor
  - British 52
  - Harquebusier 16
- Bollock dagger 41
- Bomber's badge 42
- Bonnet à poil (bearskin cap) 24
- Bonnet de police (French forage cap) 43
- Bootlace 56
- Boots 36-37
  - Bucket top 17, 36
  - Carabinier 23
  - Chinese court official 14, 36
  - Confederate Army 35
  - French infantryman 43
  - German NCO 43
  - German Panzer troops 50-51
  - Hungarian grenadier 24
  - Hussar 22
  - Indian 11
  - Jet aircrew 58
  - London Scottish battalion 42
  - Persian 10
  - Royal Flying Corps 46-47
  - Soviet sailor 56
  - Union forces 32
  - U.S. Army 53, 54
- Border 48
- Boss
  - Roman legionary 7
  - Royal Lancers' czapska 15
- Bow 41
- Suspender button 43
- Suspender strap
  - U.S. Army combat uniform 53
  - U.S. infantry equipment 44-45
- Braid
  - American army shoulder strap 27
  - Coldstream Guards 20
  - Confederate Army 34-35
  - German NCO 43
  - Hungarian grenadier 24
  - Hussar 37
  - Indian armored boot 37
  - Union forces' kepi 32
- Brass buckle 56
- Brass button 38
- Brass-covered cuirass 22
- Brass mail 10
- Brass shoulder title 42
- Brass studs 11, 37
- Bread can 45
- Breastplate
  - English knight 8-9
  - Harquebusier 16-17
  - Indian 11
  - Persian 10
  - Pikeman 16
  - Samurai 12
- Breath 48
- Breathing tube 49
- Breeches
  - Carabinier 23
  - Coldstream Guards 20
  - Confederate Army 35
  - French fusilier 25
  - French grenadier 21, 24
  - Hussar 22
  - Musketeer 16
  - Panzer Grenadier Regiment 51
  - Parliamentarian 16
  - Royal Flying Corps 47
  - Royal Navy 28-29
  - Royalist 17
  - Swiss Guard 14
- Brevet 47
- Brigandine armor 10
- Brim
  - Austrian officer's hat 19
  - North Vietnamese helmet 55
  - Pikeman's pot 16
  - Royal Navy sennet hat 19
  - Spanish helmet 18
  - Women's Royal Naval Service hat 19
- British airborne forces 52
- British army 15, 38, 46
  - Badges 27
  - Battledress blouse 38
  - Boots 36-37
  - Epaulet 26
  - Lightweight tunic 38
  - Service dress 38
  - Webbing belt 41
- British cavalry 19, 20, 26
- British colonies 20
- British hussar 37
- British infantry 20
- British medals 30-31
- British private 42
- British Royal Air Force 58
- Britain's Royal Navy 15, 27, 28
- British Royal Tank Regiment 19
- British "Sam Browne" belt 40
- British tank crewman 49
- British uniform 14
- Brog (pricker) 41
- Bronze button 38
- Bronze helmet 18
- Brow band 7, 18
- Brush 20-21
- Bucket-top boots 17, 36
- Buckle
  - British bandolier 41
  - British battledress 38
  - British flying boots 37
  - British webbing belt 41
  - Confederate Army 35
  - English knight 8-9
  - French fusilier 25
  - French infantryman 43
  - German face mask 49
  - German marching boots 37
  - German NCO 43
  - German Panzer troops 50-51
  - Harquebusier's backplate 17
  - Hussar 22-23
  - Indian accoutrements 41
  - Jet aircrew garter 59
  - London Scottish battalion 42
  - North European personal gear 41
  - Pikeman's backplate 16
  - Roman 6-7
  - Royal Flying Corps 46-47
  - Royal Navy shoe 29
  - Romanian respirator 49
  - "Sam Browne" belt 40
  - Soviet sailor's belt 56
  - Union forces 32
  - U.S. gas mask 45
  - U.S. infantry equipment 45
  - Vietcong 55
- Buckskin breeches 22-23
- Buff coat 17
- Bullet bag
  - German 40
  - Musketeer 16
- Bullet pouch 40
  - Indian accoutrements 41
- Bullions 26, 29
- Burgonet (helmet)
  - German 18
  - Italian 48
- Burma War medal bar 31
- Bursting grenade badge 24
  - British epaulet 26
  - French epaulet 26
  - Italian cap badge 27
- Butt
  - American infantry 21
  - Coldstream Guards 20
  - Confederate Army 35
  - French grenadier 21
- Butterfly crest 18
- Butterfly spur leather 17
- Button
  - American infantry 21
  - Belgian service dress 38
  - British battledress 38
  - British epaulet 26
  - British service dress 38
  - Coldstream Guards 20
  - Confederate Army 34-35
  - Czechoslovakian army 52
  - French combat jacket 53
  - French general's hat 15
  - French grenadier 21, 24
  - French infantryman 43
  - German bullet bag 40
  - German Panzer troops 50-51
  - Hungarian grenadier 24
  - Hussar 23
  - Indian army 39
  - Italian shoulder strap 27
  - London Scottish kilt 42
  - Musketeer 16
  - Royal Australian Navy 56
  - Royal Canadian Navy 56
  - Royal Flying Corps 46-47
  - Royal Lancers 15
  - Royal Navy 15, 28-29
  - Royal Netherlands Marine 56
  - Royalist officer 17
  - Soviet sailor 56-57
  - Union forces 32
  - U.S. Navy captain 56
  - U.S. submarine captain 56
- Buttonhole
  - Belgian service dress 38
  - British army shoulder strap 27
  - Confederate Army 34
  - French epaulet 26
  - French fusilier 25
  - Royal Navy 29
  - Soviet sailor 57
- By-knife 41

C

- Caligae (Roman sandals) 6
- Camouflage 38, **52-53**
  - Vietnam War 54
- Canon 8-9
- Canvas boot upper 37
- Canvas gaiter 33
- Canvas-top boot 36
- Cap
  - Badges 26-27
  - Bearskin 20, 24
  - Confederate Army 34
  - French infantryman 43
  - French Lancer 18
  - Glengarry 42
  - Indian army 39
  - Italian badge 26-27
  - New York Volunteer 33
  - Panzergrenadier Regiment 51
  - Royal Netherlands Marine 56
  - Soviet sailor 56
  - U.S. Navy captain 56
  - U.S. submarine captain 56
  - USSR Armored Unit 19
- Cap chain 40
- Cap plate 19
- Cap ribbon 56
- Cape 17
- Caped overcoat 32-33
- Capote (French overcoat) 43
- Captain's cuff stripes 23
- Captain's rank insignia 47
- Carabinieri 27
- Carabiniers **22-23**
  - Epaulet 26
- Carbine
  - Confederate Army 35
  - New York Volunteers 33
  - Royalist 17
  - Vietcong 55
- Cargo pocket 54
- Carrying case 49
- Carrying handle 7
- Carrying strap 45
- Cartridge belt 44-45
- Cartridge box
  - American infantry 21
  - Coldstream Guards 20
  - French grenadier 21
  - French navy 28
  - Russian grenadier 24
  - Union forces 32
- Cartridge pouch
  - French infantryman 43
  - German NCO 43
  - Hussar 23
  - Indian 11
- Cassack 17
- Caucasian powder charges 40
- Cavalry
  - Bell-top shako 19
  - British 20
  - Confederate Army 34-35
  - Epaulets 26
  - French 22
  - Union forces 32
- Cavalryman
  - New York Volunteers 33
  - Roman 6
- Ceremonial dress **14-15**
- Chahar ᶜaina (Persian breastplate) 10
- Chain
  - British cavalry helmet 20
  - Caucasian cap 40
  - North African 40
  - Royal Lancers' czapska 15
- Chamois leather sleeve 17
- Chape
  - North European personal gear 41
  - Roman sword 7
- Charge box 16
- Cheek piece
  - German close helmet 48
  - Pikeman's pot 16
  - Roman helmet 6-7, 18
  - Spanish helmet 18
  - Three-bar pot 17
- Chemical warfare 48
- Chenille (carabinier helmet crest) 23
- Chest defense 14
- Chevrons
  - British service dress 38
  - London Scottish battalion 42
  - Sergeant 33
  - Union forces 32
  - U.S. sergeant 54
- Chilta hazar masha (coat of ten thousand nails) 11
- Chin chain 15
- Chin scales
  - British shako 19
  - French dragoon helmet 19
  - German helmet 18
  - Hussar's shako 22
- Chin stay 19
- Chin strap
  - British shako 19
  - French czapska 19
  - Jet aircrew helmet 59
  - New York Volunteers 33
  - Pikeman's pot 16
  - Union forces' kepi 32
  - U.S. Army combat uniform 53
- Chinese armor 10-11
- Chinese court official 14, 36
- Civil War
  - American 19, 27, 32, 34, 44
  - English 16
- Civilian shirt 35
- Civilian wear 16
- Clasp 14
- Claymore mine pack 54
- Cloth bandolier 54
- Cloth boot 10
- Cloth "slide" 26
- Cloth strap 26
- Coat
  - American infantry 21
  - Armor 11
  - British infantry 20
  - Carabinier 23
  - Chinese 10
  - Coldstream Guards 20
  - Confederate Army 34
  - French army 15
  - French fusilier 24-25
  - French general 15
  - French grenadier 21, 24
  - French infantry 42
  - French navy 28
  - Harquebusier 17
  - Royal Navy 15, 28-29
  - Union forces 32
  - U.S. Navy captain 56
- "Coat of ten thousand nails" 11
- Coattail
  - French fusilier 25
  - French general 15
  - French grenadier 24
  - Royal Navy 15
- Cockade
  - American bicorn hat 19
  - American infantry 21
  - Coldstream Guards 20
  - French czapska 19
  - French fusilier 25
  - French general 15
  - French grenadier 21
  - German helmet 18
  - Hungarian grenadier 24
  - Hussar 22
  - Royal Navy hat 29
  - Russian grenadier 24
- Cocked hat
  - American infantry 21
  - Coldstream Guards 20
  - French 14
  - Royal Navy 28-29
- Coldstream Guards 20
- Collar
  - Belgian service dress 38
  - British battledress 38
  - British infantry coat 20
  - Confederate Army 34-35
  - French combat jacket 53
  - French fusilier 25
  - French grenadier's coat 24
  - Harquebusier's buff coat 17
  - Hungarian grenadier 24
  - Hussar's jacket 23
  - Indian army uniform 39
  - Persian mail shirt 10
  - Royal Flying Corps 46-47
  - Royal Navy 15, 28
  - Royalist's linen shirt 17
  - Samurai sword 13
  - Scottish service dress 42
  - Soviet sailor 56-57
  - Union forces coat 32
- Collar badge 26
  - British service dress 38
- Collar patch
  - Belgian service dress 38
  - French infantryman 43

German NCO 43
German Panzer troops 50-51
German Waffen-SS 27
Collar plate 7
Comb
  English knight 9
  German helmet 48
  Italian burgonet 48
  Pikeman's pot 16
  Three-bar pot 17
Combat badge 54
Combat helmets 18
Combat uniform 38, 52-53
Companion of the Order of the Indian Empire 31
Condiment can 45
Confederates 34-35
Continental Army 20-21
Contra-epaulet 24, 26
Cooking utensils 44-45
Cord
  Austrian officer's hat 19
  French fusilier's shako 25
  Hussar's barrel sash 22
  Hussar's shako 22
  Japanese helmet 18
  New York Volunteers 33
  Samurai armor 12-13
  USSR Armored Unit cap 19
Cotton drill 38
Court official 14
Couter 8-9
Couter wing 9
Cover
  German bullet bag 40
  U.S. entrenching tool 45, 54
  U.S. helmet 54
  Women's Royal Naval Service hat 19
Cowskin pack 25
Cravat 22-23
Crescent 26
Crest
  Carabinier's helmet 23
  French dragoon officer's helmet 19
  Headwear 18
Croix de Guerre 31, 43
Cross 30
Cross band 7
Cross of Valor 31
  Crossbelt 20-21
Crossed swords
  British epaulet 26
  French medal 31
  German medal 31
  Russian order 30
Crown
  British epaulet 26
  British medal 31
  British sabretache 41
  British shoulder strap 27
  Italian shoulder strap 27
  Prussian medal 31
  Royal Navy sennet hat 19
  Royal Tank Regiment beret 19
  Spanish medal 31
Cuff
  Belgian service dress 38
  British battledress 38
  Confederate Army 35
  Czechoslovakian army jacket 52
  English knight 9
  French combat jacket 53
  French general 15
  German combat jacket 53
  Harquebusier's gauntlet 17
  Indian army uniform 39
  Royal Flying Corps 46-47
  Royal Navy 28-29
  Royal Netherlands Marine 56
  Royalist shirt 17
  Soviet sailor 56-57
Cuff patch
  Carabinier 23
  French grenadier 24
Cuff strap 58
Cuff stripes 22-23

Cuff title 50-51
Cuirass
  Carabinier 22-23
  Indian 11
  Roman 6-7
  Samurai armor 12-13
  Swiss Guard 14
Cuisse
  English knight 8-9
  German leg armor 36
Cup 45
Czapska
  French lancer 18-19
  Royal Lancer 14-15
Czechoslovakian army 52

D

Dagger 40
  North European 41
  Roman 6
Daisho (samurai swords) 12
Damascened gold decoration 10
Dastána (vambrace) 10-11
Das Reich division 27
Death's head badge 20
Death's head emblem 50
Decoration
  English armor 8-9
  German close helmet 48
  German helmet 18
  Hussar's belt 23
  Indo-Persian helmet 18
  Italian visor 48
  Persian armor 10
  Persian helmet 49
  Pikeman's breastplate 16
  Royal Navy 15
  Spanish helmet 18
Defense Medal 30
Denim collar 57
Desert boot 53
Desert camouflage 52-53
Devil's horn 18
Dhofar (action bar) 31
Dish 44
Distinguished Service Medal 30
Diver's badge 27
Divisional badge
  British battledress 38
  South Vietnamese army 52
Do (samurai cuirass) 12-13
Dolman (short jacket) 22-23
Dolphin
  German burgonet 18
  Italian visor 48
  Roman greave 7
Donsu (samurai silk damask) 12
Doublet
  London Scottish battalion 42
  Swiss Guard 14
Dragon decoration 11, 14
Dragoon officer 19
Drawstring
  Czechoslovakian army jacket 52
  French combat jacket 53
  U.S. Army combat jacket 53
Dress bicorn hat 19
Dress coat
  Nelson's 28
  Royal Lancers' 15
Dress uniform
  British army 15
  French army 15
  French grenadier 24
  Royal Navy 29
Drill 38-39

E

Eagle
  American shoulder strap 27
  Austrian hat 19

German helmet 18
German Waffen-SS badge 27
Hussar 22-23
New York Volunteer's belt 33
Polish medal 31
Prussian helmet 27
Union hat 19
U.S. cap badge 27
U.S. medal 30
Ear guard 7
Ear roll 46
Earphone 58-59
Edge
  English armor 8
  German burgonet 18
  German leg armor 36
  Persian breastplate 10
  Pikeman's pot 16
  Spanish helmet 18
Edging
  Epaulett 26
  German trousers 50
  Hussar's boot 37
  Indian boot 37
Egyptian War-Wound medal 31
Elastic 46-47
Elbow gauntlet 16-17
Emblem
  First World War tank 19
  French czapska 19
  French grenadier 24
  German army 50-51
  Roman 6-7
Embossed decoration
  German burgonet 18
  Italian visor 48
  Roman cuirass 7
  Spanish helmet 18
Embroidered badge 26
Embroidery
  British epaulet 26
  Chinese armor 11
  Chinese court dress 14
  French general's coat 15
  Persian armor 10
  Royal Lancers' czapska 15
Enamel cross 30
Enamel rose 31
Enfield bayonet 45
Enfield revolver 41
English armor 8-9
English Civil War 16
Engraving 7
Entrenching tool 44, 54
Epaulets 26-27
  Carabinier 23
  French general 15
  French grenadier 21, 24
  French navy 28
  Royal Navy 28-29
  Union forces 32
Etching 9, 48
Evzone 14
Eye 23
Eyepiece
  Masks and faceguards 49
  U.S. gas mask 45

F

Fabric backing
  Chinese armor 11
  Samurai arm defense 13
Face defense 13
Face masks 48-49
  British splinter mask 49
  German respirator 49
  Royal Flying Corps 46
Faceguards 48-49
  English armor 8-9
  Italian burgonet 48
  Persian helmet 49
  Three-bar pot 17
Facing
  American infantry coat 21
  British infantry coat 20
  Carabinier's coat 23
  Coldstream Guards' coat 20
  Confederate Army coat 35
  French fusilier's coat 25
  French grenadier's coat 21, 24

Falkland Islands Defence Force 27
Fall fly
  Hussar's breeches 23
  Royal Navy breeches 28
  Soviet sailor 57
Falling buff 8
False collar 47
False pocket
  French fusilier 25
  French grenadier 24
  Hussar 22-23
Fastener
  British epaulet 26
  U.S. gas mask 45
Fastening
  Czechoslovakian army jacket 52
  French accoutrements 43
  French combat jacket 53
  French grenadier coat 24
  German combat jacket 53
  Indian army uniform 39
  London Scottish battalion kilt 42
  North Vietnamese shorts 55
  Roman sword strap 7
  Royal Navy breeches 28
  Soviet sailor's belt 57
  U.S. Army combat jacket 53
Feather 19
Feldbluse (German field service tunic) 51
Feldmütze (German field cap) 50
Felt hat
  Harquebusier 16-17
  New York Volunteers 33
Felt top boots 37
Fermeli (Greek tunic) 14
Ferrule 13
Festoon 19
Fez 33
Fiber button 38
Field armor 8
Field bandage
  U.S. infantryman 44-45
  Vietcong 55
Field cap 50
Field officer 26
Field tunic 43, 51
Filter
  German respirator 49
  Romanian respirator 49
  U.S. gas mask 45
Finger lame 8-9
Finnish War Medal 31
Firearms 40-41
First aid kit 59
First World War 42-43
  Badges 26-27
  Belts 40-41
  Boots 37
  Face masks 48-49
  Khaki 38
  Pack 44-45
  Tank emblem 19
Flag 13
Flange
  Pikeman's breastplate 16
  Roman armor 7, 18
Flash-pan cover 16
Flasks 40-41
Fleece lining 46-47
Fleur-de-lys 31
Flight 41
Flight Suit 58
Flintlock musket 25
Flounder
  French czapska 19
  Three-bar pot 17
Fly 47
Fly button
  Hussar's breeches 23
  Soviet sailor's trousers 57
  Union trousers 32
Fly front
  Confederate Army trousers 34
  German trousers 50-51
  Indian army uniform 39
Flying boots 36-37
  Jet aircrew 59
  Royal Flying Corps 47

Flying coat 46
Flying gauntlets 47
Flying goggles 46
Flying helmet
  Jet aircrew 58-59
  Royal Flying Corps 46
Flying trousers 58
Fob watch pocket 51
Footstrap
  French fusilier 25
  Hussar 22
Footgear 36-37
Forage cap
  Confederate Army 34
  French infantryman 43
  New York Volunteers 33
Fork 44-45
Formation badges 26-27
Foul-weather cuff
  German combat jacket 53
  U.S. Army combat jacket 53
Fourragère (lanyard) 43
Foustanella (Greek kilt) 14
Fragmentation grenade 54
French army 15, 27, 44
French carabinier epaulets 26
French cavalrymen 22
French combat jacket 53
French forces 20, 32
French Foreign Legion 53
French fusilier 24-25
French grenadier 24
French hussar 22-23
French infantry
  Epaulets 26
  Equipment 44
  First World War 42-43
  Fusilier 25
  Grenadier 21
French lancer 18-19
French navy 28
French orders 30-31
French paratrooper 53
Fringe
  French epaulet 26
  French grenadier 24
  Indian army uniform 39
  London Scottish battalion kilt 42
Fringeless contra-epaulet 24, 26
"Fritz" helmet 53
Frock coat
  Confederate Army 34
  New York Volunteers 33
  Union forces 32
Frog
  French accoutrements 43
  German powder flask 40
  "Sam Browne" belt 40
Frogged jacket 23
Fuchi (samurai sword ferrule) 13
Fukigaeshi (samurai helmet) 13, 18
Fur lining 46
Fusiliers 24-25

G

Gaiter
  French fusilier 25
  French grenadier 21, 24
  New York Volunteer 33
Gaitered trousers 21
Galea (Roman helmet) 6
Galons (cuff stripes) 22-23
Garter
  Greek Evzone 14
  Jet aircrew 58-59
  London Scottish battalion 42
  Swiss Guard 14
Garter sash 16
Gas cartridge container 59
Gas mask
  German NCO 43
  U.S. infantry 45
  Vietcong 55
Gattari (samurai flag bracket) 13
Gauntlet
  Confederate Army 35
  English armor 8-9

Harquebusier 17
New York Volunteers 33
Royal Flying Corps 46-47
General Service Medal 31
George Washington medal 30
German armor 36
German army 50-51
  Camouflage 52
  Combat jacket 53
  Face mask 49
  Medal 31
  NCO 43
  Uniform 42
  Waffen-SS 27
German bullet bag 40
German burgonet 18
German civilian respirator 49
German helmets 18, 48
German powder flask 40
German sallet 48
G-force 58
Gilded decoration
  English knight 9
  German visor 48
Gilded spur 37
Gilt band
  Harquebusier's gorget 17
  Persian helmet 49
Gilt buckle 51
Gilt button
  Royal Navy 28
  Soviet sailor 57
Gilt metal 10
Gilt plate
  Union forces belt 32
Gilt plume holder 15
Gilt stud 23
Gipser (pouch) 41
Girdle plate 7
Gladius (Roman sword) 6-7
Glengarry cap 42
Glove
  Jet aircrew 58
  Persian 10
  Pikeman 16
Goatskin knapsack 20
Goggles 46
Gold braid
  Hussar's boot 37
  Royal Tank Regiment beret 19
Gold bullions
  British cavalry 26
  Royal Navy 29
Gold collar patch 50-51
Gold decoration
  French general 14
  Persian armor 10
Gold lace
  French general 15
  Hussar 22-23
  Royal Lancer 15
  Royal Navy 15, 28-29
  U.S. Navy captain 56
Gorget
  English armor 8-9
  Harquebusier 16-17
  Italian burgonet 48
  Parliamentarian 16
Gorget patch 38
Gorget plate 9
Greave 36
  English knight 9
  German leg armor 36
  Roman 6-7
  Samurai armor 12-13
Greece 14
Greek Evzone 14
Grenade
  "Baseball" grenade 54
  Smoke grenade 54
  Stick grenade 43
  U.S. infantry 45, 54
  Vietcong 55
Grenade badge 24
Grenadiers 24-25
  British 20
  French 21, 24
  Hungarian 24
  Regiment 43
  Russian 24
Grille 48
Grip
  British sword 40
  Roman sword 7
Groin defense 14

"Grossdeutschland" Panzer grenadier regiment 51
Grotesque visor 48
Ground forces 50-51
Guard
  British sword 40
  Roman dagger 6
  Roman sword 7
  Samurai sword 13
Guard star
  German helmet 18
  Prussian helmet 27
Guerrillas 54
Gulf War 27, 52
Gunpowder 40
Gurkha hat 38
Gusset 9

H

Habaki (samurai sword collar) 13
Habit (French coat)
  Carabinier 23
  Grenadier 21
  Grenadiers and fusiliers 24-25
Hackle 19
Haft 41
Haidate (samurai lower thigh defense) 12
Halberd 16
Hammer and Sickle
  Sailor's belt 56
  USSR cap 19
  USSR order 30
Hamon (samurai sword edge) 13
Hand defense 12-13
Hand grenade 45
Handle
  Jet aircrew lifejacket 59
  Roman helmet 7
Hardee felt hat 33
Harquebusiers 16-17
Hasp 8-9
Hasta (Roman spear) 6
Hat
  Austrian Kaiserjäger officer 19
  Bicorn 21
  Civilian 18
  Coldstream Guards 20
  Confederate Army 34-35
  Felt 17
  French army 15
  French general 14
  French grenadier 21
  French navy 28
  Harquebusier 17
  New York Volunteers 33
  Royal Navy 19, 28-29
  South Vietnamese army 52
  U.S. Army combat uniform 53
  Vietcong 55
  Women's Royal Naval Service 19
Haversack
  French infantry 43, 44
  U.S. infantry 44
Headgear 18-19
  American Revolution 20
  Badges 27
  Lancer 14
  Royal Flying Corps 46
Heel
  Footgear 36-37
  German boots 50-51
  Jet aircrew boot 59
  Royal Flying Corps 47
  Soviet sailor's boot 56
  Union forces boot 32
Heel plate 37
Helmets 18
  British cavalry 20
  Chinese court official 14
  English knight 9
  German 42
  German knight 48
  German NCO 43
  Harquebusier 16

(Helmets continued)
Headgear 18-19
Imperial Gallic 6
Indian 11
Jet aircrew 58
North Vietnam infantryman 55
Persian 10, 49
Pikeman 16
Pith 55
Roman 6
Royal Flying Corps 46
Samurai 12-13
Steel 42
Swiss Guard 14
U.S. Army 53, 54
Hercules engraving 7
Hessian boot 37
Hilt
Carabinier's saber 23
French grenadier's sword 21, 24
French infantryman's bayonet 43
Hungarian grenadier's sword 24
Hussar's saber 22
Roman dagger 6
Russian grenadier 24
Samurai sword 13
U.S. bayonet 45
Hinge
English arm harness 9
German close helmet 48
German leg armor 36
Italian sabaton 36
Persian breastplate 10
Pikeman's breastplate 16
Roman armor 7
Three-bar pot 17
Hishinui-ita (samurai plate) 12
Hitler's army 50-51
Ho Chi Minh sandals 55
Hodden gray kilt 42
Hoheitsabzeichen (German national emblem)
Badge 27
Hitler's army 50-51
Holsters 40-41
Confederate Army 35
New York Volunteers 33
Panzer grenadier regiment 51
Honors
Battle honor 27
Medals and orders 30-31
Hood
Czechoslovakian army jacket 52
Romanian respirator 49
U.S. Army combat jacket 53
Hook
British sabretache 41
French infantry equipment 44
Hussar's jacket 23
Pikeman's breastplate 16
Roman armor 7
U.S. infantry equipment 44-45
British cavalry helmet 20
British shako 19
Coldstream Guards 20
Sporran 42
Hose
London Scottish battalion 42
Swiss Guard 14
Hungarian grenadier 24
Hunting horn 19
Hussars 22-23
Boots 37

Hussar's belt decoration 22-23
Imperial Gallic helmet 6-7
Imperial German officer's helmet 18
Imperial Guard 24
Imperial Russian order 30
India General Service medal 31
Indian armor 10-11
Indian armored boot 37
Indian arrows 41
Indian bow 41
Indian cuirass 11
Indian firearm accoutrements 41
Indian mail hood 48
Indian powder flask 40
Indian quiver 41
Indian Rajput armor 11
Indian shoulder defense 10-11
India-rubber cover 44
Indo-Persian helmet 18
Infantry
Confederate Army 34
First World War 42-43
French epaulet 26
German army 50-51
Pikemen 16
Roman 6
Infantryman
Confederate Army 34-35
Continental Army 21
Equipment 44
French 24, 43, 44
New York Volunteers 33
Insignia 18, 26-27
British 38
Confederate Army 35
German army 50, 53
Royal Flying Corps 47
Royal Lancers 15
Royal Navy 15
Royal Netherlands Marine 56
Union forces 32
U.S. Navy captain 56
Iron Cross 31, 51
Iron mail 10
Iron plates 6
Issue marking 52
Ita (samurai plate) 12-13
Italian carabinieri 27
Italian helmets 48
Italian infantry badge 26
Italian medical officer's shoulder strap 27
Italian sabaton 36

J

Jacket
Belgian service dress 38
British army 38
British infantry 20
Confederate Army 35
Czechoslovakian army 52
French combat 53
French navy 28
Hungarian grenadier 24
Hussar 22
New York Volunteers 33
Royal Flying Corps 47
Russian grenadier 24
Union forces 32
U.S. combat 53
Japanese helmet 18
Javelin 6
Jefferson bootee 33
Jet aircrew 58-59
Jibba (Sudanese coat) 10-11
Joint 9
Jumper 56-57
Jungle boot 54
Jungle camouflage 52
Vietcong 54
Jungle fatigue uniform 54
Jungle hat
South Vietnamese army 52
Vietcong 55

K

Kabuto (samurai helmet)
Samurai warrior 12-13
Headgear 18
Kabuto-no-o (samurai helmet cord)
Samurai warrior 13
Headgear 18
Kaiserjäger officer's hat 19
Kake-o (samurai shoulder cord) 13
Kaman (Indian bow) 41
Kamfbinde (SS armband) 50
Kamr (Indian belt) 11
Kamuri-ita (samurai plate) 12
Kashira (samurai sword pommel) 13
Katana (samurai sword) 12-13
Kepi
Confederate Army 34
French 18
Union forces 32
Khaki uniforms 38-39
North Vietnamese 54
Khanda (Indian sword) 11
Khunjar (curved dagger) 31
Kilt 42
Greek Evzone 14
London Scottish battalion 42
Kincob (Persian decoration) 10
King George VI Medal 30
King's cipher 30
Kissaki (samurai sword point) 13
Knapsack 44
American infantry 21
Coldstream Guards 20
Knee fastening
Indian army uniform 39
Royal Navy breeches 28
Knee guard 7
Knee strap
English knight's cuisse 9
Royal Flying Corps' boot 47
Knife
Infantry equipment 44-45
Jet aircrew 58
North European personal gear 41
Vietcong 55
Knight 8-9
Footgear 36
Masks and faceguards 48-49
Knot
British saber 41
British "Sam Browne" belt 40
Carabinier 23
French grenadier 24
French·navy 28
Hungarian grenadier 24
New York Volunteers 33
Russian grenadier 24
Knuckle-duster guard 45
Knuckle plate 8-9
Koftgari (Persian gold decoration) 10
Kohire (samurai shoulder pad) 12
Korean action bar 31
Korporaal (Netherlands corporal) 56
Kosaru (samurai loop) 12
Kote (samurai arm defense) 12-13
Krossia (Greek apron) 14
Kulah khud (Indo-Persian helmet)
Armor 10
Headgear 18
Masks and faceguards 49
Kulah zirah (Indian mail hood) 48
Kullah (Indian army cap) 39
Kurigata (samurai sword loop) 13

Kurta (Indian army tunic) 39
Kusari (samurai mail) 12-13
Kusazuri (samurai upper thigh defense) 12

L

Lace
British epaulet 26
British sabretache 41
Hungarian grenadier 24
Hussar 22-23
Royal Navy 28-29
Laces
Field service boot 37
Jet aircrew boot 59
Roman sandal 6
Lacing
German breeches 51
Harquebusier's coat 17
Jet aircrew 58-59
Royal Flying Corps breeches 47
Samurai armor 12-13
Lame
English armor 8-9
German helmet 18
German leg armor 36
Italian sabaton 36
Three-bar pot 17
Laminated cuisse 8-9
Laminated hand 17
Lance 8
Lance rest 8
Lancer 19
Lanyard
French infantryman 43
Jet aircrew 59
London Scottish battalion 42
Lapel
American infantry 21
British infantry 20
Coldstream Guards 20
French fusilier 24-25
French grenadier 21, 24
Royal Navy 29
Laurel-leaf
British sabretache 41
Confederate Army 35
French medal 31
German medal 31
U.S. medal 30
Women's Royal Naval Service hat 19
Leather
Armor articulation 8
Bootlace 50
Buff coat 16
Face mask 49
Flying coat 46
Gaiter top 33
Greave covering 13
Helmet 20, 42
Heel 37
Inner sleeve 17
Reinforcement 22
Sandal 6
Sole 37
Spur 17, 23
Stock 21
Leather strap
English armor 8
German belt 51
Harquebusier's backplate 17
Pikeman's backplate 16
Roman cuirass 6
Leather sword knot 40-41
Leather upper 37
Lebel rifle 43
Leg armor 36
Légion d'Honneur
Hussar 22
Medals and orders 30-31
Leopardskin turban 19
Lever 40
Lifejacket 58-59
Life-support system 58
Light 59
Light Dragoons 20
Light field armor 9
Light Infantry Brigade 54
Lightning flash 27
Linen shirt
Parliamentarian 16

Royal Navy 28
Royalist 17
Linen stocking 16
Lining
Belgian service dress 38
British battledress 38
Confederate Army jacket 34
Czechoslovakian army jacket 52
French grenadier's coat 24
French infantryman's trousers 43
Hussar's breeches 23
Indian army uniform 39
London Scottish battalion kilt 42
Persian breastplate 10
Royal Flying Corps' clothes 46-47
Soviet sailor's pocket 57
Union forces' trousers 32
Lining rivet 17, 48
Lion
British medal 31
British sabretache 41
Hussar's belt buckle 22
Royal Lancers' czapska 15
Lobate hinge 7
Lock
American infantry 21
Coldstream Guards 20
French grenadier 21
London Scottish battalion 42
Long sword
Roman 6
Samurai 12-13
Long-tailed coat 20
Loop
British bandolier 41
Field service boot 37
German marching boot 37
German trousers 50
Hussar's belt 23
Hussar's sabretache 22
London Scottish battalion kilt 42
Samurai armor 12-13
Soviet sailor 57
Loop rivet 16
Lorica segmentata (Roman cuirass) 6-7

M

M-16 rifle 54
M1910 U.S. infantry equipment 44-45
M1917 Enfield bayonet 44-45
Mabezashi (Japanese helmet peak)
Headwear 18
Samurai warrior 13
Machete 55
Magazine 55
Mail
Armor 10
Faceguards 48-49
Glove 10
Hood 48
Middle Ages 8
Persian 10
Roman 6
Samurai 12-13
Mail curtain
Indian 11, 48
Indo-Persian helmet 18
Persian 10, 49
Mameluke-hilted saber 41
Maltese cross 19
Map pocket
Jet aircrew 58
Royal Flying Corps 46
Marianne 31
Marines 56
Mars engraving 7
Mascot pin 42
Masks 48-49
Jet aircrew 59
Oxygen 58
Royal Flying Corps 46
Match cord 16

Matchlock musket
Indian 11
Musketeer 16
Mauser rifle 43
Médaille Militaire 43
Medal of Honor 30
Medal ribbon
British tunic 38
Medals and orders 30-31
Royal Flying Corps 47
U.S. submarine captain 56
Medals 30-31
Royal Navy 15
Medieval knight 8-9
Mempo (samurai face defense) 12-13
Mess kit 45
Microphone 58-59
Mine packs 54
Minerva
Medals and orders 30
Roman greave 7
Miniature medals 30
Miter caps 24
Mittens 46-47
Mizu-nomi-no-o (samurai cord) 13
Monmouth cap 16
Monster's face 48
Montero cap 16
Morian helmet 18
Motto 50
Mouche 21
Mold 26
Mouthpiece 49
Muchi-sashi-no-ana (samurai slit for riding cane) 12
Muna-ita (samurai breastplate) 12
Mune (samurai sword blade) 13
Musket
American infantry 21
Belts, holsters, and scabbards 40
Coldstream Guards 20
Confederate Army 35
French fusilier 25
French grenadier 21
French navy 28
Hungarian grenadier 24
Indian 11
New York Volunteers 33
Parliamentarian 16
Russian grenadier 24
Musket rest 16
Musketeer 16

N

Napoleon 24
Napoleonic emblem 19
Napoleonic Wars
Hussars and carabiniers 22
Nelson's navy 28
National badges 18
National cockade 21
National costume 14
National emblem 27
National Socialist Party 50
Nationale Volkes Armee 53
Naval forces 56-57
Navy badge 26
Neck chain 40
Neck flange
Headwear 18
Roman 6-7
Neck flap 52
Neck guard
Chinese court dress 14
German officer's helmet 18
Indian mail hood 48
Samurai helmet 13
Three-bar pot 17
Neck lame 18
Neck opening 11
Neckerchief 17
Nelson, Horatio 28-29
Nelson's navy 28-29
Net 18-19
New York Volunteers 32-33
Nock (Indian arrow) 41

Nonregulation breeches 22-23
North African powder flask 40
North European gear 41
North Vietnam army 54-55
Nose guard
Indian helmet 11
Indo-Persian helmet 18
Persian helmet 10
Nose valve 49

O

Oak-leaf
British shako 19
French general's coat 15
French medal 31
U.S. medal 30
USSR Armored Unit cap 19
Observer's brevet 47
Ocreae (Roman greaves) 6-7
Officer
American 19
British 15, 20, 37, 40
Carabinier 23
French dragoon 19
French grenadier 24
French lancer 19
Harquebusier 17
Hussar 22-23
Italian infantry 26
Kaiserjäger 19
Naval 56
Royal Flying Corps 46-47
Royal Lancers 15
Royal Tank Regiment 19
USSR Armored Unit 19
Women's Royal Naval Service 19
Officer of horse 17
Oil can 55
Oman General Service Medal 31
Orders 30-51
Of the Bath 14-15, 26, 29
Of the Crescent 29
Of the Garter 15
Of the Indian Empire 31
Of Maximilian 15
Of the Red Star 30
Of St. Anne 30
Of St. Ferdinand 29
Of St. Hermenegildo 31
Of St. Joachim 29
Of St. Louis 30-31
Of St. Vladimir 30
Ordnance badge 56
Ornament 20-21
Orris cord 15
Ostrich feather 19
Otayori-no-kugi (samurai stud) 13
Overcoat
French fusilier 25
French infantryman 43
Hungarian grenadier 24
Russian grenadier 24
Union forces 32-33
U.S. infantry 44-45
Overjacket 58
Overseas service chevrons 42
Oxygen mask 58-59

P

Packs 44-45
ALICE 54
French fusilier 25
Hungarian grenadier 24
Palm 31
Pantaloons
Hungarian grenadier 24
Indian army uniform 39
Panzer Grenadier Regiment 51
Panzer troops 50-51

Panzerjacke (German jacket) 50
Papier mâché skull 15
Parachutist's badge 56
Paratrooper 53
Parliamentarian 16
Partisan 14
Pauldron 8-9
Peak
  Confederate Army kepi 34
  English helmet 9
  German helmet 18
  Hungarian bearskin 24
  Japanese helmet 18
  Montero cap 16
  Samurai helmet 13
  Three-bar pot 17
Peakless cap 56
Peg 48
Pegasus 27
Pendant 6
Percussion cap
  Confederate Army 35
Percussion musket 35
Persian armor 10
Persian helmet 49
Personal equipment
  Packs and gear 44-45
Personal Equipment Connector 58-59
Pewter button 16-17
Pickelhaube (Prussian helmet) badge 27
Picker 20-21
Pike 16
Pikeman's pot 16
Pikemen 16-17
Pilum (Roman javelin) 6
Pin
  French medal 31
  German burgonet 18
  German leg armor 36
  London Scottish battalion kilt 42
  Pikeman's breastplate 16
Piping
  British infantry 20
  Confederate Army 34-35
  French grenadier 24
  French infantryman 43
  German army 50
  German Waffen-SS shoulder strap 27
  Italian shoulder strap 27
  New York Volunteers 33
  Royal Lancers 15
  Union forces 32
  USSR Armored Unit cap 19
Pistol
  French navy 28
  New York Volunteers 33
Pistol pocket 53
Pith helmet 55
Pivot
  German close helmet 48
  German powder flask 40
  German sallet 48
  North African powder flask 40
  Pikeman's breastplate 16
  Three-bar pot 17
Pizhuan (Chinese sleeve) 14
Plate
  Armor 8-9, 10
  Bearskin 27
  British shako 19
  Chinese armor 11
  French czapska 19
  French fusilier's shako 25
  French grenadier 24
  German leg armor 36
  Hungarian grenadier 24
  Indian 11
  Italian sabaton 36
  Middle Ages 8
  New York Volunteers' belt 33
  Roman 6-7
  Samurai 12-13

Plated shoulder strap 16
Pleated cloth 20
Plume 18
  American bicorn hat 19
  British shako 19
  Chinese court official 14
  Confederate Army 35
  French 14, 19, 24
  Hussar 22
  Indian mail hood 48
  Persian helmet 49
  Royal Lancers 15
  Russian grenadier 24
  Swiss Guard 14
Plume holder
  British shako 19
  French dragoon helmet 19
  Indian helmet 11
  Indian mail hood 48
  Indo-Persian helmet 18
  Persian helmet 10, 49
  Pikeman's pot 16
  Roman helmets 7, 18
  Spanish helmet 18
Pocket
  Belgian service dress 38
  British army 38
  British infantry coat 20
  Confederate Army 34-35
  Czechoslovakian army jacket 52
  French combat jacket 53
  French infantryman 43
  German combat jacket 53
  Hussar 22-23
  Indian army uniform 39
  Jet aircrew 58-59
  London Scottish battalion kilt 42
  Royal Flying Corps 46-47
  Royal Navy 28-29
  Royal Netherlands Marine 56
  South Vietnamese army 52
  Soviet sailor 57
  Sudanese coat 11
  U.S. army 53, 54
Poleyn
  English armor 9
  German leg armor 36
Polish horsemen 18
Polish medal 31
Pommel
  British sword 40
  English sword 9
  Roman sword 6-7
  Samurai sword 13
Pompom
  Fusilier 24-25
  Grenadier 21
Poncho 54
Pope's Swiss Guard 14
Pot helmet 16-17
Pouch 40
  British webbing belt 41
  French infantryman 43
  German NCO 43
  Indian firearm accoutrements 41
  North European personal gear 41
Powder charge 40
Powder flask
  German 40
  Indian 11, 41
  North African 40
Powder measure 40
Presidential Palace, Athens 14
Pricker 40-41
Priming flask 16
Provisional Sailor's Battalion 28
Prussian crown 18
Prussian Guard 27
Prussian Iron Cross 31
Pugari (Indian army turban) 39
Pugio (Roman dagger) 6
Purl embroidery 15
Purple Heart 30
Puttee 42-43

Q
Queen's South Africa medal 30-31
Quillon
  English knight 9
  French infantryman's accoutrements 43
Quiver 40-41

R
Radio homing device 59
"Raindrop" pattern jacket 53
Rajput armor 11
Rak (Indian armored boot)
  Armor 11
  Footgear 37
Rank badge
  American Union 19
  British army 38
  Panzer Grenadier Regiment 51
  Royal Flying Corps 46
Rank braid 43
Rank chevrons 32
Rank insignia
  British army 38
  Confederate Army 34-35
  German Democratic Republic 53
  Royal Flying Corps 47
  Royal Lancers 15
  Royal Navy 15
Rank star
  British shoulder strap 27
  Union forces 32
Red star
  Soviet sailor cap 56
  USSR Armored Unit cap 19
Redcoat 20
Regimental badge
  British service dress 38
  Glengarry cap 42
  London Scottish battalion 42
Regimental buckle 42
Regimental button
  British service dress 38
  London Scottish battalion service dress 42
Regimental citation lanyard 43
Regimental initials 26
Regimental number
  French fusilier's coat 25
  French infantryman 43
  Hussars' sabretache 22
Reich's cockade 18
Reinforced heel 37
Reinforced stitches 36
Respirator 48-49
Ribbon 30
  American bicorn hat 19
  British army 38
  Glengarry cap 42
  Panzer Grenadier Regiment 51
  Royal Flying Corps 47-48
  Royal Navy sennet hat 19
  Royalist 17
  Women's Royal Naval Service hat 19
Riding boot 36
Riding breeches 22
Rifle
  Finnish medal 31
  French infantryman 43
  German NCO 43
  U.S. Army 53, 54
  USSR order 30
Rifled barrel 35
Rim
  English gorget 8
  German close helmet 48
  Roman cuirass 7
Ring
  British "Sam Browne" belt 40
  Hussar 22-23

London Scottish battalion belt 42
Roman armor 6-7
Rivet
  English armor 8-9
  German leg armor 36
  German officer's helmet 18
  Harquebusier's gauntlet 17
  Italian closed burgonet 48
  Pikeman's armor 16
  Roman cuirass 7
  Spanish helmet 18
  Three-bar pot 17
Roman army 6-7
Roman helmet 18
Roman legionary 6-7
Romanian respirator 49
Rope sole 36
Roped edging 26
Rose 31
Roundel 48
Rowel 9
Royal Air Force 58
  Boots 37
Royal Armoured Corps 38
Royal arms 15
Royal Australian Navy 56
Royal Canadian Navy 56
Royal Engineers 46
Royal Flying Corps 46-47
Royal Lancers 14-15
Royal Navy 28-29
  Badges 27
  Ceremonial coat 15
  Full dress uniform 29
  Officer 56
  Sennet hat 19
Royal Netherlands Marine Corps 56
Royal Tank Regiment 19
Royalists 16-17
Rubber face mask 49
Rubber hood 49
Rubberized canvas case 49
Russian grenadier 24
Russian order 30

S
Sabaton
  English knight 9
  German leg armor 36
  Italian 36
Saber
  British 41
  Carabinier 23
  Confederate Army 35
  Hussar 22
  New York Volunteers 33
Sabretache
  British 41
  Hussar 22
Sage-o (samurai cord) 13
Saihai-no-kwan (samurai loop) 12
St. Edward's crown 19
Sallet 48
"Sam Browne" belt 40
Samurai warrior 12-13
Sandal
  Ho Chi Minh 55
  Roman 6
Sash
  Confederate Army 35
  Hussar 22
  New York Volunteers 33
  Order of the Garter 15
  Parliamentarian 16
  Royalist 16-17
  Union forces 32
Saya (samurai scabbard) 13
Scabbards 40-41
  American infantry 21
  British 40-41
  Carabinier 23
  Confederate Army 35
  French grenadier 21, 24
  French infantry 43
  Hussar 22
  Indian 11
  Jet aircrew 58
  New York Volunteers 33
  Roman 6
  Samurai 13
  U.S. infantry 45

Scale 26
Scarf
  French grenadier 21
  French infantry 43
  French navy 28
  North Vietnamese 55
  Vietcong 55
Schirmmütze (German officer's cap) 51
Scots Greys Regiment 26
Scottish units 42
Scutum (Roman shield) 6
Second Anglo-Afghan War 30
Second World War
  Boots 36-37
  British belt 41
  Camouflage 38, 52
  German forces 50
  Insignia 27
  Medals 30-31
  Respirator 49
  U.S. helmet 18-19
Sennet hat 19
Sequins 10
Serpent 16
Service chevrons 38
Service dress 38, 42
  Belgian army 38
  British jacket 38
  First World War 42
  Khaki 38
  London Scottish battalion 42
  Royal Flying Corps 46
Service flash 38
Shako
  British cavalry 19
  French fusilier 24-25
  Hussar 22
  Russian grenadier 24
Shagreen binding 36
Sheath 41
Shell jacket 34-35
Shield
  Finnish 31
  Roman 6
Shikoro (samurai neck guard) 13
Shirt
  American infantry 21
  Coldstream Guards 20
  Confederate Army 35
  French navy 28
  Greek Evzone 14
  Harquebusier 17
  Musketeer 16
  North Vietnam infantry 55
  Pikeman 16
  Royal Navy 28
  Royal Netherlands Marine 56
  South Vietnamese army 52
  Soviet sailor 56-57
  U.S. Navy captain 56
  U.S. submarine captain 56
  Vietcong 55
Shoe
  American infantry 21
  Coldstream Guards 20
  Confederate Army 35
  French fusilier 25
  French grenadier 21, 24
  French military 36
  French navy 28
  New York Volunteers 33
  Pikeman 16
  Royal Air Force 37
  Royal Navy 29
  Royal Netherlands Marine 56
  Russian grenadier 24
  U.S. submarine captain 56
Shoe tie 36
Shoelace 37
Short sword
  Roman 6
  Samurai 13
Shorts 55
Short's patent knapsack 44
Shot 40
Shoulder cord 13
Shoulder defense
  Chinese armor 11, 14
  Indian 10-11
  Samurai 12
Shoulder harness 54

Shoulder pad 12
Shoulder plate
  Roman 6-7
  Samurai 12
Shoulder strap
  American army 27
  Belgian service dress 38
  British army 27, 38
  Confederate Army 34
  French combat jacket 53
  French fusilier 25
  French infantryman 44
  German combat jacket 53
  German Waffen-SS 27
  Harquebusier's backplate 17
  Indian army uniform 39
  Italian army 27
  Jet aircrew 58
  London Scottish battalion 42
  Parliamentarian 16
  Persian armor 10
  Pikeman 16
  Royal Flying Corps 46
  Royal Lancers 15
  Royal Navy 15
  Royal Netherlands Marine 56
  Russian grenadier 24
  "Sam Browne" belt 40
  U.S. Army combat jacket 53
  Vietcong 55
Shoulder title
  British battledress 38
  London Scottish battalion 42
Shozoku-no-o (samurai shoulder cord) 13
Shutzstaffel (SS) 50
Side plate 10
Siegrunen (German victory runes)
  Collar patch 27
  Hitler's army 50
Sight
  English falling buff 8
  German helmet 48
  Indian mail hood 48
  Italian burgonet 48
Signal flares 59
Signal mirror 59
Silk cockade 29
Silk damask 12
Silk lacing 12
Silk lining 15
Silk pad 26
Silk sash 32
Silk tab 15
Silver crescent 26
Silver lace
  British shako 19
  British epaulet 26
Skirt
  English knight 8
  French infantryman's overcoat 43
  Persian armor 10
  Royal Flying Corps' coat 46
  Royal Lancers' dress coat 15
  Royal Navy coat 29
  Sudanese coat 11
Skull
  French dragoon helmet 19
  German burgonet 18
  German close helmet 48
  German sallet 48
  Persian helmet 49
  Pikeman's pot 16
  Royal Lancers' czapska 15
  Spanish helmet 18
  Three-bar pot 17
Slashed breeches 14
Slashed doublet sleeve 14
Sleeve
  Chinese court official 14
  Confederate Army 34-35
  Harquebusier's buff coat 17
  North Vietnamese shirt 55
  Persian mail shirt 10

Roman 6
Royal Navy shirt 28
Royalist 17
Soviet sailor 56-57
Sudanese coat 11
Swiss Guard 14
Union forces 32
U.S. Navy captain 56
Sleeve band 27
Sleeve insignia 26
Slider 41
Sling
  British sabretache 41
  Carabinier 23
  Coldstream Guards 20
  Confederate Army saber 35
  French fusilier 25
  French grenadier 21
  Hussar's sabretache 22
  New York Volunteers 33
  Union forces 32
Slipper 14
Slouch hat
  Union Army 19
  Confederate Army 34-35
Smoke grenades 54
Snap-sack 16
Sneck-hook
  English armor 8-9
  Italian burgonet 48
Sock 33
Sode (samurai shoulder defense) 12-13
Sole
  British flying boot 37
  Chinese court official 36
  German boot 37, 50-51
  Indian armored boot 37
  Jet aircrew's boot 59
  Persian boot 10
  Roman sandal 6
  Soviet sailor's boot 56
  Union forces' boot 52
  U.S. infantryman's boot 54
South Vietnamese army 52, 54
Soviet navy 56-57
Soviet sailor 56
Spanish medal 31
Spanish morion helmet 18
Spathae (Roman long swords) 6
Spatterdash 20
Spear 6
Spike
  German helmet 42
  Indian helmet 11
  Indo-Persian helmet 18
  Italian burgonet 48
  Persian helmet 10
Splinter mask 49
Sponge mouthpiece 49
Spoon 44-45
Sporran 42
Spout 40
Spring 40
Spring-loaded stud 8
Spur
  Confederate Army 35
  English knight 9
  Harquebusier 17
  Hussar 22, 37
Spur leather
  Carabinier 23
  Harquebusier 17
Spur slot 36
Spur step 37
Square-toed boot 17, 36
SS
  Hitler's army 50
  Insignia 27
SS Schütze (private) 50
Star
  1914-1915 47
  1939-1945 30
  American slouch hat 19
  British epaulets 26
  British service dress jacket 38
  British shoulder strap 27
  British star 30
  Carabinier's cuirass 23
  French medal 31
  Hussar's belt decoration 23
  Italian shoulder strap 27

(Star continued)
Order of the Bath 14-15, 26
Order of the Garter 15
Prussian helmet 27
Royal Flying Corps officer's jacket 47
Royal Navy epaulet 28-29
Union forces 32
U.S. Navy officer 56
U.S. submarine captain 56
Stars and Stripes 53
State of New York belt buckle 33
Steel cuirass 22
Steel helmet
French infantryman 43
German NCO 43
Headgear 18-19
U.S. infantrymen 54
Steel pot helmet 16
Steel sole 54
Stick grenade
German NCO 43
Vietcong 55
Stock
American infantry 21
Coldstream Guards 20
French navy 28
Royal Navy 29
Stocking
Coldstream Guards 20
Greek Evzone 14
Royal Navy 29
Stopper 40
Stop-rib 8
Strap 40
American infantry 21, 44
Belgian service dress 38
British bandolier 41
British boot 37
British epaulet 26
British shako 19
Confederate Army 34-35
English armor 8-9
French czapska 19
French equipment 44
French fusilier 25
French infantryman 43
German burgonet 18
German marching boots 37
German respirator 49
Hussar 22
Indian army uniform 39
Indian quiver 41
London Scottish battalion kilt 42
Musketeer 16
Persian armor 10
Pikeman 16
Roman 6-7
Romanian respirator 49
Royal Flying Corps 46-47
Royal Navy epaulet 29
Russian grenadier 24
Union forces' epaulets 32

U.S. gas mask 45
U.S. helmet 19
U.S. infantry equipment 44-45, 54
Vietcong 55
Strap loop 15
Straw hat 19
Stripe
British service dress 38
Egyptian medal 31
New York Volunteers' trousers 33
Royal Navy ceremonial coat 15
Royal Navy Vice-Admiral's coat 29
Royal Netherlands Marine 56
Stud
English armor 8-9
German grotesque visor 48
German marching boots 37
Harquebusier's breastplate 17
Hussar's belt 23
Indian armored boot3 7
Indian cuirass 11
Italian closed burgonet 48
Italian sabaton 36
Persian armor 10
Pikeman's breastplate 16
Royal Flying Corps officer's jacket 47
Samurai face defense 13
Studded cloth 10
Submarine service 56
Sudanese military coat 10-11
Sugake odoshi (samurai lacing) 13
Suigyu-no-wakidate (samurai helmet ornament) 13
Suit of armor 8
Suneate (samurai greaves) 13
Survival kit 59
Swag 7
Swan's feathers 15
Swan's neck hook 41
Swastika
Badge 27
Hitler's army 50
Swiss Guard 14
Sword
British "Sam Browne" belt 40
Carabinier 23
English knight 9
Finnish medal 31
French grenadier 21, 24
French medal 31
French navy 28
German medal 31
Indian 11
Musketeer 16
Roman 6-7
Royalist 17

Russian grenadier 24
Russian order 30
Samurai 12-13
Swiss Guard 14
Sword baldric
Indian 11
Royalist 17
Sword belt
French grenadier 21
Hussar 22
Musketeer 16
Union forces 32
Sword decoration 26
Sword emblem 6
Sword knot
British saber 41
Hussar 22
Sword strap 7

T

Takahimo (samurai cord) 12
Tang 15
Tank crewmen 48-49
Tank troops 50
Tank wheels 27
Tape
British splinter mask 49
London Scottish battalion puttee 42
Tarkash (Indian quiver) 41
"Tarleton" helmet 20
Tartan lining 42
Tassel
American bicorn hat 19
British bearskin 20
British shako 19
Chinese court official 14
French fusilier 25
French grenadier 24
Greek Evzone 14
Hussar's barrel sash 22
Hussar's boot 37
Japanese helmet 18
New York Volunteers 33
Persian helmet 49
Persian mail shirt 10
Royal Navy hat 29
Sporran 42
Union forces sash 32
Tasset
English knight 9
Pikeman 16
Tateage (samurai plate) 12
Tekko (samurai hand defense) 12-13
Tent 44
Terminal
Persian breastplate 10
Roman sword 7
Thigh defense 12
Thigh plate 11
Three-bar pot 17
Throat strap 18
Thunderbolt 22-23

Tie
Indian cuirass 11
Persian armor 10
Roman cuirass 7
Roman helmet 18
Royal Netherlands Marine 56
U.S. Navy captain 56
U.S. submarine captain 56
Tie strap 37
Tinsel 10
Tir (Indian arrow) 41
Toe caps 36-37
Toe lame 9
Toe plate 9
Toggle
Hussar's barrel sash 22
Linen shirt 17
Tomb of the Unknown Soldier, Athens 14
Tong huxiang (Chinese neck guard) 14
Tonghu xinjing (Chinese chest defense) 14
Tongkui (Chinese helmet) 14
Tongxing (Chinese rivets) 11
Tongxing ding jia (Chinese coat armor) 11
Tongxing hubo (Chinese shoulder defense) 11, 14
Tongxing pizhuan (Chinese arm defense) 11
Top (Indian helmet) 11
Torador (Indian musket) 11
Torch 53
Tosei gusoku (samurai armor) 12
Totenkopfabzeichen (German death's head emblem) 50
Tourie 42
Trade badges 26-27
Soviet navy 57
Trench knife 45
Tricker guard 16
Tricolor plume 14-15
Tricorn hat 19
Troop inscription 7
Trooper 55
Trophy of Arms 26
Trousers
American infantry 21
Anti-G 58
Confederate Army 34-35
French infantry 42-43
French navy 28
German NCO 43
German Panzer troops 50
New York Volunteers 33
Royal Netherlands Marine 56
Russian grenadier 24
South Vietnamese army 52

Soviet sailor 56-57
Union forces 32
U.S. Army uniform 53, 54
U.S. Navy captain 56
U.S. submarine captain 56
Vietcong 55
Tsarouhia (Greek slipper) 14
T-shirt 53
Tsuba (samurai sword guard) 13
Tube
Caucasian powder charges 40
German face mask 49
U.S. gas mask 45
Tunic
Greek Evzone 14
Indian army uniform 39
Roman 6
Royal Flying Corps 46
Turban
Faceguard 48
Khaki 39
Turnback
American infantry coat 21
British infantry coat 20
French fusilier's coat 25
French general's coat 15
French grenadier's coat 21, 24
Turned edge
English knight's gauntlet 8
Roman cuirass 7
Tire sole 55

U

Undress uniform 28
Union Army 27
Union eagle 19
Union forces 32-33
Unit badge 53
United Nations' Korea medal 31
Urban camouflage 52
U.S. Forces
Air Force 27
Armored Division 27
Combat uniform 53
Infantry 44, 54
Medals 30
Navy captain 56
Officer's cap badge 27
Steel helmet 19
Submarine captain 56
U.S.-pattern belt 52

V

Vambrace
English 8-9
Indian 11
Persian 10

Velcro
French combat jacket 53
Jet aircrew clothing 58-59
U.S. Army combat jacket 53
Victoria Cross 30-31
Victory medal 31
Victory runes
Collar patch 27
Hitler's army 50
Vietcong 55
Vietnam War 54-55
Virginia Cavalry 34-35
Visor
Helmets 48
Jet aircrew 58-59
Voltigeurs 24

W

Waffenfarbe (German piping) 50
Waffenrock (German field tunic) 43
Waffen-SS
Camouflage 52
Hitler's army 50
Waist belt 40
Waist flange 8
Waist strap
Harquebusier 17
Jet aircrew 58
Pikeman 16
Sporran 42
Waistcoat
Coldstream Guards 20
French fusilier 25
French grenadier 21, 24
French navy 28
Hussar 22-23
New York Volunteers 33
Royal Navy 28-29
Wakizashi (samurai sword) 12-13
War in Vietnam 54-55
Wars
American Civil War 19, 27, 32, 34, 44
American Revolution 20-21
Burma 31
English Civil War 16
First World War 19, 26-27, 37, 38, 40-41, 42-43, 44-45, 48-49
Gulf War 27, 52
Napoleonic Wars 22, 28
Second World War 27, 30-31, 36-37, 38, 41, 44, 49
Vietnam War 54-55
Washington, George 30
Washington shield 30
Watagame-no-yoko-ita (samurai backplate) 13
Water bottle 44-45
Confederate Army 35
French infantry 43
U.S. infantry 45, 53, 54
Vietcong soldier 55

Weapons
Harquebusiers and pikemen 16
Middle Ages 8
U.S. anti-tank 54
Weatherproof cuff 52
Webbing belt 41
Whistle
Jet aircrew lifejacket 59
London Scottish battalion 42
Wilhelm Ernst War Cross 31
Women's Royal Naval Service 19
Woollen fringe 26
Woollen sock 33
Woollen tunic 6
Worsted sash 32-33
Wound stripe
British service dress 38
Egyptian medal 31
Wreath
Union hat 19
German emblem 50
Medals 31
Royal Tank Regiment beret 19
Union forces' kepi 32
Women's Royal Naval Service hat 19
Wrist band 17
Wuguanzhi Zhurizhuang (Chinese court official) 14

X

Xiongjia (Chinese groin defense) 14

Y

Yodare-kake (samurai throat defense) 13
Yurugi-ito (samurai lacing) 12

Z

Zipper
British flying boots 37
Jet aircrew 58
Zirah (Persian mail shirt) 10
Zouave uniform 32-33

Acknowledgments

Dorling Kindersley would like to thank:
Diana Condell, M.J.R. Allen, and the staff and the Trustees of the Imperial War Museum, London; David Edge and The Wallace Collection, London; Christopher Gravett, and the Board of Trustees of the Armouries; Musée de l'Empéri, Salon de Provence; The Museum of Antiquities of the University and Society of Antiquaries of Newcastle-upon-Tyne; Andrew Cormack and The Royal Air Force Museum, Hendon, London; Spink and Son Ltd., London; David Spence, Tina Chambers, Admiral of the Fleet, The Lord Lewin, KG GCB LVO DSC, and the staff at the National Maritime Museum, Greenwich, London;

D.F. Harding, London; G. W. Harding, York; Mark Dennis, London; Alan Turton, English Civil War Society, Basing House; Michael Butler Collection; J. Craig Nannos, US Consultant, Ardmore, Pennsylvania; Gettysburg National Military Park, United States National Park Service; The Civil War Library and Museum, Philadelphia, Pennsylvania; USS Olympia Association, Philadelphia, Pennsylvania; Dale E. Biever, Boyertown, Pennsylvania; Andrew L. Chernack, Springfield, Pennsylvania; C. Paul Loane, Cherry Hill, New Jersey; Lawrence R. Schmidt, Burlington, New Jersey; Sergeant Feliciano, Philadelphia,

Pennsylvania; Sergeant Mike Smith, Jonestown, Pennsylvania; Robert McDonald, Cherry Hill, New Jersey.

Additional editorial assistance:
Fiona Courtenay-Thompson, Roger Tritton, Edwina Johnson.

Additional photography:
Peter Chadwick, London; Phil Kramer, Philadelphia, Pennsylvania.

Index:
Jane Parker.